THEN AND THERE SERIES
GENERAL EDITOR
MARJORIE REEVES

The France of Louis XIV

W. K. RITCHIE

Illustrated from contemporary sources

LONGMAN

LONGMAN GROUP LIMITED
London
*Associated companies, branches and representatives
throughout the world*

First published 1977
ISBN 0 582 20540 9 .

Printed in Hong Kong by
Sheck Wah Tong Printing Press

To Scott Allan

Contents

To the Reader

What was so special about the France of Louis XIV? These stamps

should tell you. They show famous French people who lived in Louis' reign: the writers, La Fontaine, Molière and Madame de Sévigné, and the statesmen, Colbert and Louvois. These were only a few of the many clever people who lived in France at this time. You would be right in thinking that there must have been something special about the reign of Louis XIV. It was the longest reign in European history, seventy-two years, from 1643 to 1715 (longer even than Queen Victoria's from 1837 to 1901). A famous historian described Louis himself as 'the ablest man who was born in modern times on the steps of a throne'. To his court came all the great writers, artists and scholars of France. He made France the world's leading country. Everybody wanted to copy French fashions and French became the language of all educated people. This book tells you about the successful first half of the reign, from 1643 to about 1685. But it is not only about Louis and other famous people, it is also about the ordinary people of France, the peasants in the country and the towns-folk of Paris. They too made France great in the time of Louis XIV.

Words printed in *italics* are explained in the Glossary on page 94.

1 'The Dregs of the People'

Of the 18 million people who lived in France at this time 15 million were peasants. This means that most French people, eight out of ten, worked on the land.

The kind of farming they went in for depended on where they lived, for as you know France is a land of great contrasts in climate and soil. In the seventeenth century the contrasts in the way people lived in different parts of France were much greater than they are now. The size and shape of the farmers' fields, the kind of plough they used, the amount of taxes they paid, and even the language they spoke, varied greatly between one part and another. This was because France was a kingdom made up of many provinces that had come together at different times, each with its own laws and customs that were all quite different.

Even so, there were many things that French peasants had in common, no matter where they lived. Most of them had some land on which to work; only a few were *serfs,* which means that most could leave the land and work somewhere else if they chose. About a tenth of French peasants were wealthy enough to employ servants and to afford small luxuries. Most, however, had only enough land from which to scrape the barest living. All had to pay taxes and make various kinds of other payments to their landlords, for although it was the peasants who farmed the land less than half of it actually belonged to them. The rest belonged to people who did not work the land themselves: townsfolk, nobles, the Church and the King. Also, peasants' land was usually the poorest in a district and was divided up into scattered plots instead of forming compact holdings. 5

This map of France shows you the old provinces and those parts added during Louis XIV's reign, as well as places mentioned in the book

Everybody knew that work on the land made France rich, but the peasants were still known as 'la lie du peuple', 'the dregs of the people'.

6   Let us take a look at the way some peasants lived in that

fertile part of northern France known as the Île de France which has Paris at its centre. Imagine you are travelling through this countryside in the middle of the seventeenth century. Picture a flat, gently rolling landscape, with broad open fields without walls or hedges, stretches of meadowland and clumps of woodland, crossed by roads that are dusty white tracks in summer and rutted mudpatches in winter. Every so often you come to a small village, made up, perhaps, of only a few white-washed cottages at the side of the road, with a church and school nearby. Farther back from the road, through a break in

French peasants at home. Notice their clothes and the food on the table. What else tells you that these are fairly well-off people?

the trees, you may just catch a glimpse of a high wall with tall gates and a house with a tower and a *weather-vane*.

The people we have come to see have no towers or weather-vanes on their houses. They live in simple cottages made of either wood or *wattle and daub* and roofed over with thatch. A hole in the wall serves as a window, and if we peep in we can see that the floor of the cottage is made of beaten earth. Some cottages consist of only one room, with a stone partition separating it from the cowshed. Behind the house is a garden for growing a few cabbages, some *hemp*, beans and peas. Hens cluck and flutter everywhere at our approach, setting off the ducks and geese down by the village pond.

No one is about. Everybody is busy in the fields beyond the village. The fields belong to the whole village, and each farmer has his share of several strips on which he grows his crops. The chief crop is wheat, but they also grow millet, oats and rye. So fertile is the soil that they can grow more than one crop a year. They take care not to exhaust the soil by leaving one field *fallow* every two or three years to let the goodness return. It is on this grassy fallow ground that the villagers graze their few cattle

Peasants in the fields. How many kinds of farm-work can you see going on? What tells you that this is a scene in the north and not the south of France?

and sheep. Those who farm up on the hillsides keep more sheep which feed on the excellent pasture. On the southward-facing hillsides they also grow vines.

Some houses in the village are bigger, more solidly built and better cared-for than the rest. Obviously these are the homes of better-off peasants. When these men register the birth of their children with the priest, let us say, or are asked their occupation by the taxcollector, they proudly state that they are 'laboureurs' (husbandmen). This only means that they own a plough and a team of horses, but of course many own much more than that. François Andrieu is one of these wealthier peasants. He farms nearly 40 hectares and has two ploughmen to help him. He has five horses, three cows, twenty-three sheep and a couple of pigs. As a result he and his family are never afraid of going hungry because he has always enough grain, calves and wool to sell.

Very few peasants were as rich as these husbandmen. In one village of eighty-six householders only three were 'laboureurs'. In many villages there were none at all. Most French peasants were known as 'manouvriers', people who worked with their hands. In addition to working in the fields they had to take on other jobs to make ends meet because they had so little land. Let us meet one of them.

Pierre Durand lives with his family in one of the little mud huts down by the roadside. He does not spend much time in it because he is too busy working in his plot of 10 hectares, scattered in strips all over the village fields. However, he is glad he has any land to farm. Others have no land at all nor any animals either, while he has at least a skinny old cow and a few sheep. He cannot afford to keep a horse or a pig and he has only a few chickens because they eat so much. He has only a sack or two of corn to keep him and his family for a couple of months. This is why he has to do other work such as weaving to earn money for more food. Richer farmers may plough his land for him and give him some seed but he has to give them back some of his crops. He also does odd jobs for them, such as cutting their hedges, cleaning out their ditches or tending their vines. 9

More French peasants. Compare them with those on page 7. Which do you think are better-off?

Despite all their hard work Pierre Durand and his family are still miserably poor. They may sleep on the floor. Their only pieces of furniture will be perhaps a stool or two, a chest, a bench and a kneading-trough for making bread. Their food is scanty and monotonous. This is how one writer of the time describes it:

All the so-called 'bas-peuple' [lowest-class of people] live on nothing but bread of mixed barley and oats, from which they do not even remove the bran, which means that bread can sometimes be lifted by the straw sticking out of it. They also eat poor fruits mainly wild, and a few vegetables from their gardens, boiled up with a little *rape-* or nut-oil sometimes, but often not, with a pinch of salt. Only the most prosperous eat bread made of rye mixed with barley and wheat. The general run of people seldom drink wine, eat meat not three times a year, and use little salt.

This is how he describes their dress:

Winter and summer, three-fourths of them are dressed in nothing but half-rotting tattered linen, and are shod throughout the year with *sabots,* and no other covering for the foot. If one of them does wear shoes he only wears them on saints' days and Sundays.'

Can you wonder that many died of hunger and cold?

DUES AND TAXES

Many peasants might just have been able to make do if they had not had to pay out what were known as their feudal dues. These were payments, made either in cash or in goods and services, which were quite separate from rent, for even rich farmers who owned their land had to pay them. They were paid to the person who was known as the *superior* of the land. This custom dated back to medieval times when every man was supposed to have a superior or lord to protect him from other men. In the past peasants had to work for their lord so many days a year and give him a share of what they produced in return for his protection. These days were now gone: lords no longer gave their peasants protection, but peasants still had to pay their feudal dues. The superior of the land, or *seigneur,* might be the local landlord, often a nobleman, but sometimes it was a merchant in a nearby town or the nuns of a distant convent. Like everything else in France at this time, feudal dues varied even from district to district in the same province.

Let us suppose you were a French peasant. Almost certainly, wherever you lived, you would have to pay out so much money for the actual land you held. This sum had been worked out centuries before and no longer amounted to much because the value of money had fallen. Much heavier, however, were the

A peasant feeding his hens. Notice the tools he is carrying. What does he use them for, do you think? Look carefully at his livestock. How different are they from farm animals today?

payments you had to make from your produce, which could be as much as 10 per cent of all your corn. There were all kinds of other irritating little dues. Perhaps you lived in a part of the country where you had to take your corn to the lord's mill, which might be miles away from your farm; you would have to pay the miller a sixteenth part of the meal he ground for you.

Your bread might have to be baked in the lord's oven, and so you would have to pay the baker so many of your loaves he had baked. You might have to make your wine in the lord's wine-press; again a charge would be made. Wherever you travelled on the lord's estates he had the right to charge you *tolls* for using his bridges, his ferries and even the roads. On top of all these payments you still had to work for the lord in his fields, usually at harvest-time when you were busiest on your own land. And if you wanted to get out of this responsibility you would have to pay somebody else to do the work for you.

What if you defied your lord and refused to pay him any of these dues? You would be brought to trial, of course. And who do you suppose your judge might be? None other than the lord, or his representative. So you would have to carry out your duties after all, and also pay for the cost of your own trial for all the trouble you caused him!

Of all the rights that lords had over peasants the most hated was a lord's right to hunt on their land. If, let us say, you had just ploughed your field, your work would all have been in vain if the lord and his friends rode up with their hounds to go hunting; and if you put up any fences to keep them out you would get into serious trouble. But if you trapped a wild animal on your land for spoiling your crops, or snared a rabbit to eat, you could be accused of *poaching*. Until the law was changed in 1699 if you were found guilty of poaching more than twice you could be put to death.

Peasants had probably always grumbled about paying their feudal dues, but they grudged them all the more when they seemed to get nothing in return. Most of the old duties the lords used to perform, like keeping law and order, were now carried out by officials of the King.

Then, of course, after you had paid your dues you had still taxes to pay. One tax was the *tithe* which was meant to support the local priest. This was supposed to be a tenth of a peasant's property but often it amounted to much more. Other taxes were paid to the King. There was the taille, a tax on land, which in some provinces was simply what the tax-collector thought you could afford to pay. Peasants never knew how much they would have to pay. No matter how it was assessed, the taille caused endless trouble, everyone claiming that he had been charged too much.

The taille was what is known as a direct tax. There were many taxes which people paid indirectly because they were included in the price of things they bought. There was the 'gabelle', for instance, a tax on salt, something everybody had to buy for cooking and which was essential for preserving meat and fish. Finally, there were various taxes called 'aides', like our Value Added Tax today, whereby a tax was charged at every stage of making wine or cider, from the picking of the fruit to the sale of the liquor in the wineshop. On top of all these taxes and dues peasants might find themselves having to provide food and lodgings for a bunch of rowdy soldiers and not get paid a *sou* in return.

HARD TIMES AND GOOD TIMES

It was bad enough having to make all these payments in good years when corn was plentiful, but there were years on end, from 1649 to 1652 for example, when the harvest failed and famine struck. Then, thousands of people died of starvation. Many were driven to eating dogs, cats and donkeys, grass and

Soldiers wandering about the countryside did not care how badly they treated the local people

roots of trees. Even cases of *cannibalism* were reported. At the same time, perhaps in the next province there might be plenty to eat, but the people in the province where the harvest was bad might starve, so slowly did it take news to travel. But even if people did know of others' misfortune they were not always able to help because of bad roads or flooded rivers.

After famine often came outbreaks of plague, for which there was no cure. As a result of all this suffering around them people got accustomed to death. Most people died long before they reached sixty anyway, even if they were usually in good health. It has been estimated that out of every hundred children born, twenty-five died before they were even a year old, another twenty-five only reached twenty, and a further twenty-five were dead by the age of forty-five. An old man who reached eighty was looked on as a wonder and when he died the whole neighbourhood would turn out for his funeral.

Grim though village life could be there was a brighter side too. Peasants did not work all the time. Women would laugh and gossip as they did the family washing together at the river-side. The men would gather for their game of 'boules' (bowls) on the village green. Everybody joined in celebrating the many holy days and saints' days scattered throughout the calendar. Dancing was one of their favourite pastimes, as the English *philosopher*, John Locke, noted in his journal during his travels in France:

> At St Gilles a *congregation* of men and *wenches* danced heartily to the beating of a drum for want of better music; nay, their natural *inclinations wrought* so *effectually* that it helped them to dance even when the dubbing of the drum failed them.

There was much merry-making at family gatherings, weddings and birthdays. Many a lord also invited his peasants to dance on his lawn in summer and eat supper with him in his barn at harvest and at Christmas.

2 *The Favoured Few*

The seigneur and his family were the most important people in the neighbourhood. When they rode by or passed in their coach you would be careful to stand well back, the men to take off their hats respectfully and the women to bob a little curtsey. In church you would hurriedly stop talking and watch in silence as they strolled in and sat down in their special pew apart from the rest of the congregation, for the noble families of France were people apart in more ways than one.

There were about 400,000 people in France who belonged to these noble families. They owned most of the land: in Provence it was about a tenth, in Burgundy, Artois and Picardy it amounted to about a third. Owning so much land made them the richest people in France. The Prince of Condé was one of the richest. His total fortune was worth about 31 million *livres*. Most noblemen were not nearly so rich as the Prince of Condé. Some were only a little better-off than their own peasants, with only one estate worth about 500 livres which they worked themselves. Most, however, were comfortably off with around a thousand acres which brought them in an annual income of about 30,000 livres.

Just as there were rich nobles and poor nobles, so there were grand nobles and not-so-grand nobles. Members of the Royal Family, for example, regarded themselves as above all the rest. Next came those families which had been noble for centuries. They belonged to a class that was called the 'noblesse d'épée' (the nobility of the sword), whose members had received their noble rank for serving the King in battle. They looked down their noses at those nobles, known as the 'noblesse de robe' (nobility of the robe), who had received their noble title more recently for serving the King in other ways, such as being advisers or civil servants. Many of these newer families were very rich, but they were still despised by older families who might be poor but whose titles were much older. As one member of an old noble family said, 'the King could make a nobleman but not a gentleman'.

Whatever their origin all nobles had certain privileges which kept them apart from other people. Only noblemen were supposed to be allowed to carry a sword. They had also the right to display a coat of arms. They were also supposed to behave in a superior way which set them apart from ordinary people in everything they did.

A COUNTRY NOBLEWOMAN

French nobles spent most of their time on their estates. Marie de Rabutin-Chantal was one. Like the children of many nobles, however, she was born in her parents' town-house, or 'hôtel', in Paris. Her parents died when she was quite young and so she was brought up in the country, first by her grandparents and then by an uncle. Unlike children of many noble families, who went to the village school, Marie was educated at home by private tutors, who found her a very keen pupil. By the age of eighteen she could read and speak Italian, Spanish and Latin and write excellent French. Some ladies and gentlemen could hardly read or write at all.

Soon it was time for Marie to be married and so her uncle looked around for a suitable husband for her. Young men and women, even those of humble birth, were not expected to marry whom they wanted. Marriages were arranged by their parents, sometimes when the children were as young as ten or twelve. A marriage was looked on as a kind of alliance between families of the same social class. Noble parents would never dream of allowing their daughter to marry the son of a merchant or lawyer (although it did happen sometimes), just as a rich peasant would try to stop his son from marrying the daughter of a poor peasant. Marie's uncle found her a most

Marie de Rabutin-Chantal, better known as Madame de Sévigné, whose letters to her daughter tell us so much about French country life

suitable husband, a young nobleman who was handsome and rich. His name was Henri, Marquis de Sévigné, and it is by the name, Madame de Sévigné, that Marie is better known.

Madame de Sévigné was a devoted wife. Soon she was the mother, first of a son and then of a daughter. Her husband's home was at Les Rochers, near Rennes in Brittany, where she spent the summer months, moving to their town house in Paris in winter. Les Rochers was like other old country houses which had been built in more lawless days, more like a castle than a house, with its *turrets* and tiny windows. Madame de Sévigné modernised its appearance by ordering many of the trees to be cut down, planting others and laying out graceful walks and gardens.

Country houses at this time consisted of a large hall with many smaller rooms leading off from it. The walls were white-washed or covered with wooden panelling and tapestries, and decorated with swords, suits of armour and family portraits. The floors were made of bare stone or polished wood and

Madame de Sévigné's country house in Brittany. Notice the steeply-pitched roofs and turrets, which were typical of many old-fashioned country-houses in France

scattered with a few rugs. At one end of the hall there was a huge fireplace, which was stacked high with blazing logs in winter. There was not much furniture: a long table, a few high-backed leather arm-chairs, a tall cabinet and a chest or two. Upstairs in the bedrooms there was little space for anything except high four-poster beds and more chests for keeping linen. Downstairs in the basement there would be a large cool kitchen, a laundry, and cellars for storing food and drink.

Madame de Sévigné was rich enough to afford a *major-domo* to look after her house and keep an eye on the servants. Most nobles had at least one or two servants. They were often treated as members of the family and were cursed and beaten, although they usually answered back quite freely. Wages were low and paid so seldom that servants were allowed to help themselves to meat and drink. They were also supplied with clothes. One

Inside a nobleman's house, with the family gathered around the fire in winter. Notice the small panes of glass, the window-shutters, the tapestry on the walls, the plain furniture and the four-poster bed on the right

nobleman said that his servants were forever telling him that it was time he bought a new coat and handed the old one on to them. Servants in France spoke to the masters in a way that would have shocked most English noblemen at this time.

Unlike many ladies Madame de Sévigné does not seem to have been very interested in house-keeping herself. She spent her time in other ways as this letter to her daughter shows:

We get up at eight o'clock, and go to *Mass* at nine. The weather decides whether we take a walk or not, each often going his own way. We eat a good dinner. A neighbour drops in, and we discuss the news. In the afternoon we work, my daughter-in-law at a hundred and one different things, and I at two bands of tapestry. At five o'clock we separate and take a walk, either alone or together. We meet at a very lovely spot, we have books, we pray, we dream, we build castles in the air, sometimes gay ones sometimes sad. My son reads us

A lady receiving her guests while still in bed. As you can see from this and the picture opposite, there were no clear-cut differences as yet between dining-rooms, bedrooms and sitting-rooms

delightful books: we have one book of *devotion*, the others of history. They amuse us and keep us occupied. We discuss what we read. Receiving letters and answering them occupies a large part of our lives, especially in mine. We have supper at eight o'clock. They leave me at ten o'clock – I rarely go to bed before midnight.

Letter-writing must have taken up most of Madame de Sévigné's time. Sometimes she wrote three or four in one day. For thirty years she wrote letters to her many friends, and especially to her beloved daughter. They enjoyed reading all her news and gossip so much that they kept her letters and passed them round their friends to read as well.

Some nobles were so poor that they had to spend nearly all their time working in the fields like their own peasants. Indeed, but for their noble title and snobbish pride, you would hardly have been able to tell the difference. Such country gentlemen

A priest in a noble household. Many such priests were in the Church only for the money it brought them. Some led very worldly lives. This one is grinding snuff

were called 'hobereaux'. In Ireland they would have been known as 'squireens', in Scotland as 'bonnet lairds'.

Better-off nobles could afford to leave their estates in the hands of a bailiff and do whatever they liked with their time. Some spent it hunting and fishing, others went in for studying the plants and wild life of their district and looking for ancient ruins. Some set up schools and hospitals for their tenants but many seemed to do little else but over-eat, get drunk and gamble the family fortune away.

Planning their children's future would take up much of their time. Imagine you are the head of a noble family, consisting of two sons and two daughters. Your elder son, a fine strapping boy, will one day inherit the family property, but in the meantime can serve as an officer in the army. That will cost a lot. You will have to buy his *commission,* pay for his clothes and equipment, and also provide him with an allowance, because his pay won't support him. Your elder daughter, a sweet but plain child, is too old to marry now and so she will have to be sent to live in a convent. Of course, you will have to pay for her upkeep there: it is looked on as a kind of *dowry,* just as you will have to pay a dowry to the husband you have been lucky to find for your younger daughter. That just leaves your younger son. What is to happen to him? He is too timid and too delicate to join the army. Never fear, your powerful cousin at court will somehow find a *living* for him in the Church. Even if he were a proper rascal and too dull to learn a word of Latin he might still be made an *abbot.* He need not even become a priest, he will still be able to draw an income from the Church lands that go with the job. After all, there is little else that sons of noblemen can do but join the Church or serve the King. They cannot become lawyers or merchants. And daughters of noblemen must get married or become nuns. Working for their living is unheard of. And so, as a result of having to find money to pay for dowries, commissions in the army and generally keeping up appearances, most noblemen fell deep into debt. Many were therefore glad to send their sons to seek their fortune at the court of the King, as you can see in Chapter 4.

RIVIERE DE SEINE

3   A Visit to Paris

At some time or other everybody who lived in the countryside came into town. Peasants came into market to sell their chickens or vegetables and buy some salt or a new pot, while the gentry came to do their shopping, consult their lawyer, or visit the *apothecary*. Most towns were very small places with perhaps only a hundred inhabitants or so. About half-a-dozen, great trading centres like Lyons and Bordeaux and ancient provincial capitals such as Rennes and Rouen, had populations of between sixty and a hundred thousand. Altogether, about three million people, or 15 per cent of the whole population, lived in towns in France.

French towns all looked alike in some ways and most were very old. They were usually surrounded by a moat and high walls with gates, or 'portes', which were closed at dusk every night. The houses inside clustered round an old castle or stately cathedral in the middle. Nearby was the market square, from which ran off a maze of tiny lanes and narrow streets. Here and there throughout the town were other open spaces, such as churchyards, orchards and gardens belonging to convents, as well as the townsfolk's backyards behind their houses.

THE STREETS OF PARIS

By far the largest and busiest town in all France was the city of Paris. It was the largest city in Europe, with a population in

Left: *A bird's-eye view of the crowded city of Paris, looking eastwards along the river Seine. See if you can pick out the city wall with its moat and many gates, the Cathedral of Notre Dame on the Île de la Cité in the middle of the Seine, and the Bastille in the far distance*

1684 of about half a million. London's population was half as big, while Bristol and Edinburgh had each about 30,000 inhabitants.

What must it have been like to live in Paris at this time? Imagine that you have just come in from the country on your first visit and that you are going to stay with your uncle who lives in the old part of the town. Here you are at the Porte Saint Denis, one of the half-dozen city gates. It is still early morning. The gate is just opening to let in a crowd of country people who have been waiting to get into market with their carts and baskets full of fresh vegetables. There are workmen, too, hurrying in from the 'faubourgs' (suburbs) just outside the town walls. While you were waiting you looked up in amazement at these walls, two metres thick and nine metres high. Where they come down to the Seine are two tall towers from which heavy iron chains are hung to keep out enemy ships during a siege. Paris is well protected against attack.

Once inside the city you make your way along the broad *Rue* Saint Denis. Already it is busy with coaches, carts and men on horseback. Herdsmen are leading animals to market or driving them out to graze on the hills outside the town. Never before have you seen so much dirt! In some streets the mud lies nearly half a metre thick. And those smells! Down the middle of the streets run open sewers, strewn with all kinds of foul rubbish. Under the windows of the houses stand piles of steaming dung and pools of dirty water. Little wonder that travellers say that they can smell Paris before they ever see it.

As the streets get narrower and the houses higher you know that you must be getting nearer the town centre. Some of the houses are more than five storeys high. Each storey reaches farther out than the one underneath on both sides of the street until the ones at the top almost seem to touch. At times you feel you are in a long dark tunnel for the streets are only two metres wide in places. – Splash! Oogh! You press yourself against the side of a house. Someone has just thrown some evil-smelling slops out of an upstairs window!

26 The signs of the various tradesmen hanging outside their

Look at all that is going on in this lively street scene in Paris. Notice the covered pavement, the shop signs and the goods being sold in the open booths. What sounds and smells does this picture make you think of?

booths tell you that you cannot be very far now from your uncle's house. Tradesmen still live above their workshops and members of the same trade are to be found in the one street. Here is the Rue de la Chausseterie (Stocking-makers' Street), there is the Rue de la Savonnerie (Soapmakers' Street). The houses have no street numbers but a passer-by soon directs you to your uncle's house.

AT HOME IN PARIS

You are looking for a house with a little gilt bale of wool swinging at the end of an iron rod above the door. This shows that your uncle is a cloth merchant. To see the whole front of the house you have to stand well back and look up from the other side of the street. It has three storeys with an attic under its high-pitched roof of grey slate. Like others round about, it is made of brick, covered with plaster and diagonal-shaped woodwork. Its windows are set with tiny diamond-shaped panes of glass.

Your uncle and aunt are pleased to see you. He is dressed in a thick grey woollen coat and breeches, with short lace cuffs and a neat white *cravat* at his neck, thick knitted stockings and stout leather shoes. She is wearing a skirt and bodice made of wool on top of a linen underskirt, woollen stockings and leather shoes, and a linen cap on her head.

Your uncle's workshop, along with store-rooms, kitchen and laundry are all in the basement of the house. Steep, dark, narrow stairs lead up to the parlour and bedrooms on the floors above. Most of the rooms are small and dark, with walls covered with oak panelling and floors made of polished pine. On the first floor is the parlour, the largest room in the house. A tapestry hangs on the wall. This is the only form of decoration apart from a looking-glass and one or two family portraits. This room is where the family gather and take their meals at a long walnut table, sitting on high-backed chairs covered with leather or flowered tapestry. Mugs and dishes made of *pewter* are kept in the wooden dresser standing against the wall. Opposite is the blue-and-white tiled fireplace, on one side of which is a long wooden settle with a high back to keep out draughts. Upstairs are the bedrooms, crammed with four-poster beds and large wooden linen chests.

Every room in the house is occupied. The family lives on the first floor with grandparents or other relatives in rooms above.

28

*The wife of a merchant,
with her skirt
tucked up for working
around the house*

If there are rooms to spare they are let out to other families. New houses are being built in Paris but only for rich people. Poor people have to crowd into older houses.

Not only tradesmen like your uncle, but merchants, lawyers and doctors, all the people who make up what is known as the middle class live in such houses in Paris. Some middle-class people are very much richer than others, for example, *financiers* who lend vast sums of money at high rates of interest. These are the sort of people who can afford to buy those new houses now going up in the more fashionable parts of town on the outskirts. Their houses are made of stone and look like little palaces standing in their own grounds.

HOME ENTERTAINMENTS

Unlike people who had to work for their living the rich people of Paris had plenty of leisure-time and room enough in their houses to entertain their friends. They gave *lavish* dinner parties. Servants came back from market laden with baskets full of food and prepared it in the large kitchen. Much of the meat 29

Pastry-cooks in the kitchen of a large house, making pies. From the picture you can tell what is likely to be inside the pies

was stewed. Cooks would throw great chunks of beef, lamb and veal into huge copper pots and allow them to stew for hours. We would say that their food was over-cooked. Chicken, duck and game were eaten in great quantities but fish less so, although oysters, taken grilled or raw, were very popular. Fresh vegetables from local market gardens were always in good supply – cabbages, artichokes, asparagus, onions and *garlic*. They were not so much eaten fresh in salads as made into rich soups with plenty of lentils and beans. Peas were eaten fresh, however. Although great care was taken in the preparation of food much of it was stone cold by the time it reached the table because the dining-room was so far from the kitchen.

This was a time when eating habits were quickly changing. Hostesses insisted that their servants set the table properly. Separate napkins, just coming into use about 1660, could be folded in any one of thirty ways. Until this time the linen table-cloth had been used as a napkin by all the diners. It was also becoming the fashion to serve food in separate courses instead of placing all the dishes on the table at the start of the meal.

Diners were expected to follow the rules of good behaviour that they read in the many books of *etiquette* published around this time. Here are some examples:

When eating you must not eat quickly or greedily, no matter how hungry you may be, for fear of choking; in eating you must keep your mouth closed and not lap up food like an animal.

Cut up your meat into small pieces and do not make your cheeks bulge like a monkey.

Do not gnaw bones, nor break and shake them to get out the marrow. Cut your meat on the plate and then carry it to your mouth with your fork.

(Forks were just coming into use at this time).

Readers were also told that it was good manners to eat with their hat on but most ill-bred to pick their teeth with their knife when toothpicks were at hand. And if you had to spit at table it was better to turn your head away discreetly to the side. From these rules of how people were supposed to behave at table you can tell how they must have actually behaved!

After dinner was over there was time for other kinds of entertainment. Young ladies were expected to show off how well they could play the *harpsichord* or sing to the guitar. Sometimes the gentlemen went off to play billiards and joined the ladies later for a game of cards. Some ladies would be content to carry on with their embroidery, which kept them busy most of the day as well.

SIGHT-SEEING IN PARIS

Richer people also went out for their entertainment. Afternoon bathing parties held in a bath-house anchored in the river Seine were very fashionable. Bathing was also a way of keeping clean, for there were no bathrooms even in the houses of 31

A lady playing on a spinet, like a harpsichord—an early sort of piano with a more tinkling sound

the rich. Washing yourself, however, was still thought to be rather daring it seems, according to a book of the time: 'To wash in water is bad for the sight, produces toothache and catarrh, makes the complexion pale, exposing the face to cold in winter and sunburn in summer.'

Dirty or clean, however, Parisians loved to show their city off to strangers. You could get about Paris in various ways.

Right: *Use this plan of Paris to help you to find the places you read about in this chapter*

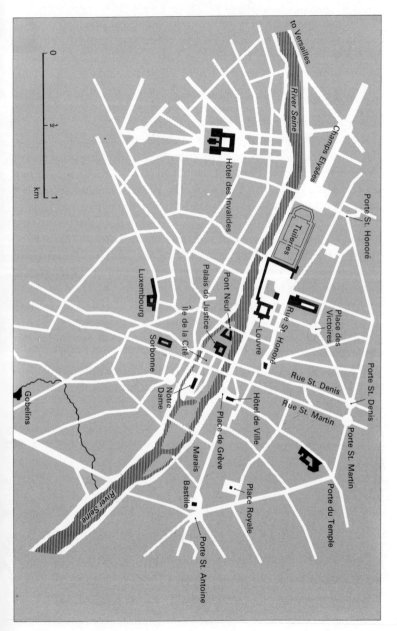

to Versailles

River Seine

Champs Elysées

Porte St. Honoré

Hôtel des Invalides

Tuileries

Luxembourg

Palais de Justice

Pont Neuf

Place des Victoires

Île de la Cité

Rue St. Honoré

Louvre

Sorbonne

Rue St. Denis

Porte St. Denis

Notre Dame

Rue St. Martin

Hôtel de Ville

Porte St. Martin

Gobelins

Place de Grève

Marais

Porte du Temple

River Seine

Bastille

Place Royale

Porte St. Antoine

0   ½   1 km

33

Your host might be very rich and lend you his private coach or perhaps hire one for you. In the 1660s you could have gone about in the coaches run by a private company along a particular route; these carried up to eight passengers. For short distances you could always hire a *sedan chair*. But like most Parisians you might put up with all the noise, the smells, the dirt and the traffic and go about on foot.

Let us start our tour of Paris in the heart of the old town, in the busy Place de Grève. The dignified building you see over there is the Hôtel de Ville (Town Hall) where the town council meets. Crowds in the Place de Grève are beginning to thin now. We must have just missed one of the sights of Paris, a public hanging. Look, the corpse is still dangling from the gibbet. Soon the crows will come along and pick out the eyes, tear off the flesh and leave another gaunt skeleton hanging in the breeze. The victim must have been just an ordinary sort of person because noblemen have their heads chopped off with an axe. Other forms of punishment are just as cruel. Ravaillac, the man who murdered King Henri IV with a dagger in 1610 not far from here, had his right hand burned off, his body torn open and the wounds filled with boiling oil, and while he was still alive his body was hauled apart by horses tied to his arms and legs. People who live in the Place de Grève let out their

A public execution

windows to spectators of such gruesome goings-on. Madame de Sévigné came here to watch the execution of a court lady who had poisoned several people, including her own father.

Shivering a little, we hurry away and come to a more modern part of town, the Place Royale. Many visitors come here to admire the new houses. They are all the same height and look like one large house with a garden in the middle. You can walk round the square under an *arcade* with fashionable shops under the houses. This is one of the first town squares ever to be built. Soon architects will copy the Place Royale and squares like it will appear in London and other cities all over Europe.

We now cross the river Seine by one of Paris's many bridges, like others in being made of wood, with houses and shops rising up on both sides. This takes us to the very oldest part of Paris, the largest of the little islands in the middle of the Seine, known as the Île de la Cité. This is where the first Parisians lived in early times. Rising up from all the crowded houses and narrow streets is the famous cathedral of Notre Dame, the most sacred church in all France, with its twin towers and spire. The beautiful stained-glass windows make it very dark inside, but by the light of hundreds of flickering candles at its many altars, we can see that it is a very busy church. People seem to come and go all the time, including students from the university who use the nave as an examination hall.

Another bustling place nearby is the Palais de Justice. The High Courts of France sit here and many people come in to listen to eloquent lawyers argue their cases before the solemn-faced judges.

It is easy to see from the haughty way they go about that lawyers are very important people. France still has many different kinds of law. Not only are there different laws for different parts of the country but there are also laws which are issued by the King, known as *edicts*, which have to be registered by important courts of law known as *Parlements*, of which the Paris Parlement is the most powerful. Apart from the Parlements there are separate courts for the Army, the Navy, the Church and even servants of the King. All these courts have

Inside a lawyer's office. The bags on the walls were for carrying documents. Notice also that lawyers were sometimes paid with food instead of cash

their own codes of law and lawyers who have been specially trained to use them. No lawyer can be expected to know all these laws, that is why there are so many lawyers in France. For all who come into contact with it the law is a nightmare, except for lawyers themselves. They make a fortune out of it. Because there are so many law courts cases take years to settle and all the while clients have to pay out fees to the lawyers who handle them. Now you may understand why there are so many proud lawyers and angry clients in the Palais de Justice.

It is refreshing to get into the open air again, but not for long because we are just beside the river bank. Down by the water's edge some housewives are wringing out their washing. Up river some men are idly fishing, but it is a wonder any fish can live in this water with all the dirty rubbish pouring into it

The ever-busy Pont Neuf, with its open booths and sideshows. The statue in the middle is of Henri IV, the king who ordered the bridge to be built. This is a view looking westwards. Notice the boats tied up at the 'quais'. On the right you can see the Louvre, that stately-looking building in the middle distance

from the city's sewers. Can we wonder that disease is common in Paris? The Seine is also a busy waterway as we see from the many small boats and barges tying up at the quais (embankments), and loading and unloading their cargoes.

We shall have to leave to another day's sight-seeing a visit to the Left Bank of the river. There you can meet students at the many colleges of the University, the most famous of which is the Sorbonne. We can make our way back to the Right Bank by crossing the Pont Neuf, the most famous of the Paris bridges. Everybody comes here and joins in the noisy, bustling crowds. 'Roll up! Roll up! Roll up!' It is like a fairground.

The Pont Neuf brings us at length to one of the most exclusive new districts of Paris, the Rue St Honoré, with its many fine houses. It is near the Louvre, the King's magnificent palace overlooking the Seine. Some time we must wander through its galleries full of beautiful pictures and statues by great artists which the King allows members of the public in to admire. They are also allowed to stroll through the pleasant gardens of another royal palace, the Luxembourg, over on the Left Bank. But we have no time to visit either of these places. Foot-sore and tired we come to the end of our tour of Paris.

4 Versailles

Paris in the seventeenth century was a very old town, but about forty kilometres away to the south-west a brand new town was springing up. At one time Versailles was a sleepy little village, with one or two inns where cattle-drovers used to drop in for a drink on their way home from market. By the end of the century it was a bustling town of wide streets with noblemen riding up and down in their carriages. And all this came about because the King built a palace there.

Louis XIV had many palaces in and around Paris but he loved Versailles the best. The Palace was started by the King's father, Louis XIII. As a keen sportsman, he wanted a hunting-lodge in the forest where he could put up for the night and yet be within easy reach of Paris. Louis XIII liked Versailles so much that he spent much of his time there and rebuilt it as a country house. Louis XIV also was fond of hunting, but he was not content with the little country house his father had built. He wanted something much grander. Extensions to Versailles were therefore started in 1661 and went on almost without stop for the next twenty years and more until it became the biggest palace in Europe.

Five men were mainly responsible for building the Palace of Versailles. Jean Baptiste Colbert, Controller-general of the King's finances, provided the money out of taxation. The expense was enormous. Clearing the site for building alone cost a fortune. One writer of the time described the site as 'the saddest and most barren of places, with no view, no wood, no

Left: *A view of Versailles in the mid-1660s, soon after it was built. See how much of the countryside round about has been turned into formal gardens*

water, and no earth, for it is all shifting sand and marsh, and the air, consequently, is bad'. Water had to be led all the way from the river Seine by means of a system of water-wheels and pipes sunk underground. Large numbers of men were employed on the clearance and building. In one month it was reported that: 'During the last month, the sum of 250,000 livres has been spent on Versailles. Every day 22,000 men and 6,000 horses were working there. There were many fatal accidents.' No one will ever know exactly how much Versailles cost to build because Louis destroyed Colbert's careful accounts, but it must have been many millions of livres.

The countryside round about was gradually transformed into the Palace grounds. These were laid out by the King's landscape gardener, André Le Nôtre. He designed the grounds at the back of the Palace to look like a vast garden, with long walks between rows of stately poplar trees and neatly trimmed yew hedges arranged in geometrical patterns known as 'parterres'. There were also ornamental lakes, canals and many fountains in the form of giant statues of gods and heroes of ancient times. To bring colour to the grounds millions of tulip bulbs were specially imported from Holland and orange trees from Spain.

Various architects helped to design the Palace itself but it was mostly the work of Louis Le Vau. He left Louis XIII's little country house of red brick and yellow sandstone untouched, and built round it outlying *pavilions* linked by long stately corridors. Le Vau designed Versailles in what is known as the Italian style of architecture; this means that the windows, columns and arches, and the forms of decoration are like those found in palaces in Italy. The whole lay-out was exact and *symmetrical*. Later additions to Versailles were on a much greater scale. Some people say that these spoil Le Vau's work because they are out of proportion with the original buildings. When the Palace was complete the garden front was about 600 metres long, nearly three times as long as the east front of Buckingham Palace.

The interior of Versailles was perhaps even more breath-taking than the outside. This was decorated by Charles Le

Inside the palace of Versailles: the grand staircase, made of grey and green marble

One of the many magnificent rooms in Versailles, with walls made of marble. It leads into the hall of mirrors on the right. Notice on the wall the large sculptured figure of Louix XIV on horseback, dressed like a Roman emperor

Brun, the King's painter-in-chief and director of the royal tapestry works at Gobelins. He designed everything to match, down to the last keyhole and doorknob. No one could fail to be impressed by the sheer grandeur of the Palace. La Fontaine, the fable-writer, exclaimed:

So many beautiful gardens and *sumptuous* buildings are the glory of the country that produces them. And what must not foreigners say! What will not *posterity* record *confronted* by this masterly achievement of all the arts combined.

Imagine what it must have been like to be shown round the Palace when it was just built. One of several stately staircases of marble would take you up to the main floor. Your feet would echo as you wandered from one gigantic chamber to the next, each more awe-inspiring than the last, and with names of ancient gods like the *Salon* of Mars, the Salon of Diana and the Salon of Apollo. You would be amazed at the decoration: brightly painted ceilings showing heroes and gods of ancient times, *friezes* and *cornices* richly encrusted with gilt, and walls that were covered with tapestries or panelled with delicate shades of cream, green, pink or blue marble. Windows were hung with thick curtains, flowered silk in summer and embroidered velvet in winter. Some of the furniture was even made of silver. At night everything shimmered and glowed in the candlelight of sparkling crystal chandeliers.

THE SUN-KING

The man who was chiefly responsible for Versailles, however, was none other than the King himself. Louis XIV supervised every stage of the building. Architects and decorators had to carry out what he wanted. In fact, Versailles is a lasting memorial to this French king.

If you go round Versailles you cannot help noticing how one particular design keeps on appearing in the decoration. You see it everywhere, in the plaster-work, on door panels and even on the garden railings, and that is the sun in all its splendour. This is no accident, for the sun was Louis XIV's personal emblem and he was known as 'Le Roi Soleil' ('the Sun King').

It is easy to see why he chose the sun as his emblem. As you know, the sun is the centre of the universe and the source of all energy. In the same way Louis XIV aimed at being the centre and source of all power in his kingdom. He wanted everybody to be under his authority. And so, just as all the planets revolved round the sun, so would everything in France revolve round him. A vast palace would show everybody how powerful a king he was.

Another reason why Louis built Versailles was that he disliked living in Paris. How he hated its dirty, narrow streets, its crumbling old buildings, but most of all its proud citizens who did not show him enough respect! Although Colbert tried hard to make him save money by living at the Louvre, Louis would not listen because he could not forget his memories of living in Paris as a boy.

Louis XIV became king at the age of five when his father died in 1643. As he was too young to rule by himself, his mother, Anne of Austria and the chief minister, Cardinal Mazarin, ruled in his name. Many powerful people, including those influential lawyers of the Paris Parlement you read about in Chapter 3, as well as many nobles, disliked the way the Queen-mother and Mazarin governed, so they rose in rebellion. The civil wars that now broke out are known as the 'Wars of the Fronde'. The French word 'fronde' means a boy's catapult, and at first the Queen and Mazarin thought that the nobles and Parlements were just like little boys firing mud and stones and making a nuisance of themselves, but they soon saw how dangerous they were.

Louis had to endure many hardships during the Wars of the Fronde. He had to go short of new clothes and put up with torn sheets on his bed to save money to pay his soldiers. But by 1652 Louis's supporters had been able to defeat the *Frondeurs* and restore peace. Gradually Cardinal Mazarin set about reducing the power of the great nobles and of the Paris Parlement. All the while Louis was determined that when he was old enough to

Cardinal Mazarin, dressed in his cardinal's cap and gown of deep red. Although an Italian by birth, he helped Anne of Austria to rule France when Louis XIV was still a boy

rule nobody in France would ever again be able to make the King afraid. He would leave Paris to its rebellious lawyers and ugly mob and live in safety at Versailles; he would make a palace that was big enough, not only for himself, but for all the members of the government along with their clerks and servants. He would make Versailles, and not Paris, the capital of France. Here he would keep an eye on his nobles by making them serve him in his everyday life and stop them plotting against him in their own castles. Louis carried out his plans. The Palace of Versailles was made bigger and bigger until finally in 1682, while masons and plasterers were still at work, Louis moved in for good, along with many of the greatest nobles in the land.

Much of the fighting in the Wars of the Fronde took place in and around Paris among small groups of soldiers. The building that you see on the right is the Bastille

LIFE AT VERSAILLES

At first many nobles did not want to come to live in the King's Palace. Before long they were begging to come, to receive one or other of the many jobs the King could offer in the army, the navy, the civil service and the Church. Some of the jobs involved a lot of hard work, but others were only sinecures, that is jobs for which you got paid for doing hardly anything at all.

Imagine that you were a young nobleman arriving at Versailles for the first time. You are a younger son, let us say, of one of those 'hobereaux' you read about in Chapter 2. Thanks to the influence of a distant relative, you are to become a page-boy to the King, although one day you hope to become an officer in the Royal Guards. Shabbily dressed though you are, you have no trouble in getting into the Palace because the sentries

A school for noblemen's children in the early seventeenth century with their schoolmaster. Even they had to be punished at times, it seems

see from the sword you are wearing that you are nobly born.

There were about 150 page-boys at Versailles. To become one you had to belong to one of the oldest noble families in France, be fifteen years old, around 1.5 metres tall and good-looking. You had also to be very sturdy because you were on duty from 6.30 in the morning until late at night, ready to run errands and perform such duties as taking off the King's boots when he came back from hunting and fetching his slippers when he went to bed. Pages had also to go to school in the Palace; as well as reading, writing and counting they had also to learn how to ride, fence and dance. They were quite well cared for: one page-boy wrote home to his mother: 'At dinner we have soup, boiled beef, four *entrées*, two roasts and four sweets.' In between spells of duty they had lots of fun. When the King was at prayers they used to climb up on to the roof of the chapel and shout rude things at the people on the ground.

As a page-boy you would live with other servants and officials in the domestic quarters over the kitchens near the Palace entrance. Some nobles lived there too. Others lodged in the town of Versailles. Some lived in the Palace itself. They must have been very crowded because their families lived there with them. About a century later somebody did a survey of the Palace and found that it contained 226 dwellings and twice as many single apartments.

Many a proud nobleman was content to live in a garret at Versailles. The Duc de Saint-Simon, who was very proud of his ancient *lineage*, tells us in his *memoirs* how he lived in three tiny rooms overlooking a nasty-smelling courtyard where the public lavatories stood. The hall of his apartment was so small he could hardly stand up straight because the space had been cut horizontally to provide cubicles for his servants. He spent much of his time in his study, a windowless closet that had to be lit by candles all day. Yet Saint-Simon was the envy of other courtiers. A royal duchess once begged him to let her use his apartments for a wedding reception because her own were too small. Nobles were willing to put up with all sorts of discomforts in order to live under the same roof as the King at Versailles.

No matter how poor they were, nobles soon learnt that they had always to appear well dressed at court. Men as well as women had to keep up with the latest fashions in clothes set by the King. Around 1660 the style of men's clothes was very decorative. It consisted of a waistcoat and loose breeches that were folded over to look like a skirt and known as 'rhinegraves'. Under the waistcoat they wore white linen shirts with long, floppy sleeves, lace cuffs and a lace cravat. Stockings were made of silk and so were the fancy bows that decorated their brightly coloured high-heeled shoes. These bows were sometimes so long that to avoid tripping themselves up men had to walk with their legs wide apart with the help of a long walking-stick. By the 1680s fashions had changed: breeches were becoming narrower, shoes simpler, while the waistcoat was worn longer with a tight-fitting coat. This was the beginning of the jacket that men wear today. Throughout the later part of the seventeenth century men wore their hair long and had wide-brimmed hats trimmed with huge feathers. Many shaved their heads and

47

A meeting of Louis XIV and his courtiers (on the left) with the King of Spain and his courtiers. Here you can see men's fashions early in the 1660s

wore wigs with masses of curls instead. Some wigs weighed as much as a kilo and were so bulky that men had to carry their hats under their arm in case they fell off.

Ladies had to pay just as much attention to their dress as men. In some ways, however, their fashions were not so elaborate as men's and changed less often in style. Ladies' costume consisted chiefly of a gown and skirts with matching bodice. The top skirt was worn very full and was set off with rows of tiny ribbons. Often it was tied back to form a train and reveal the more tightly fitting underskirts. Ladies of quality had at least three of these. The length of a lady's train indicated her rank; for example, the Queen's measured eleven *ells* and a duchess's only three. Then as now, ladies prided themselves on their narrow waists. The bodice was therefore tapered at the waist with tight corsets, laced up with silk ribbons, cut very low at the neck and finished off with short puffed sleeves. For going out of doors a lady would wear a long robe, a satin one in summer and a fur one in winter.

Hair styles changed more than costume. One that was in fashion for many years was the 'fontanges', called after Mademoiselle de Fontanges, one of the King's mistresses, who when out riding once pinned up her hair with a ribbon in the form of a turban. For a time this casual style was all the rage at court, but the Palace hairdressers soon transformed it into a most artificial creation by stretching the hair over a wire frame that could only

How a lady at court dressed early in Louis's reign

be unwound with the help of a locksmith, it was said. Just as now, ladies had many other aids to beauty, such as face creams and perfumes. For many years beauty spots were very fashionable. These little patches started out as ways of covering up smallpox scars but were later worn on different parts of the face, near the eyes, close to the lip, on the nose, and were considered very attractive indeed.

Keeping up with all these changing fashions was very costly. A nobleman's coat, for example, might cost as much as 1200   49 livres, and every so often the King would tell his courtiers to get a new one. Rather than displease him they had to obey, even if it meant borrowing more money. Noblemen prided themselves on rarely paying their debts, however, which must have been rather hard on court tailors. And yet tradesmen went on competing with each other to supply the court because of the honour and extra trade it brought them. No doubt they made up their losses by charging humbler customers all the more.

Courtiers at Versailles, showing the fashions of 1696. Notice the ladies' hair styles

Now suitably dressed, you would be able to take your place as a page-boy along with other courtiers. In many ways it must have been like early days at a new school. There were so many strange rules of behaviour at court that a newcomer must have spent his first weeks making all sorts of terrible mistakes. You learnt, for example, never to knock on a door at Versailles but to scratch it with the nail of the little finger of the left hand. And if a servant brought you a message from a nobleman of a higher rank than yourself you received it standing bareheaded. There were many other intricate rules of *precedence*. When walking in procession the King and Queen and members of the Royal Family always came in front of everybody else, followed in strict order by foreign princes, *cardinals*, dukes, lower members of nobility and finally commoners. Difficulties often arose between people who appeared to be of the same social rank; two duchesses, for instance, might quarrel over which of them should enter a room first or over what kind of seat they were allowed to sit on. There were three kinds of seats at Versailles, armchairs, chairs without arms, and footstools. So complicated were the rules about who should sit on which that ladies and gentlemen often came to blows or took each other to court over them.

THE KING'S DAY

It was the King himself who insisted on all these complicated rules of behaviour, but he was bound by them just as strictly himself. Everything he did was turned into a ceremony in which the courtiers took part.

As a courtier at Versailles you would begin your day about 7 a.m. when your *valet* roused you and helped you to dress. With hardly time to wash, you would powder and perfume yourself and hurry down to the ante-room outside the King's bedroom. Here you would join other noblemen who were waiting for the King to get up and take part in the first ceremony of the day, the 'lever du Roi' (rising of the King).

The King's day began early too, at 7.30, when a servant gently wakened him for his doctors to come in to make their daily examination. By 8.15 he was ready to receive members of the Royal Family and some of the leading nobles. They were quietly admitted into the royal bedroom to see the bed curtains drawn back for the King to wash his hands and face in a few drops of spirits of wine and then choose the wigs he intended to wear that day. Favourite members of the court were then allowed in to watch him sip his breakfast of broth or herb tea. Specially favoured courtiers were permitted to take it in turn to hand him his shirt when he was dressing. Every other day he was 51

The King's bedroom at Versailles

shaved. For a short time he would then retire to his study with his advisers. During his absence a procession of courtiers would form up for the King to lead them to Mass in the chapel. Louis was a very *devout* man: he said his prayers regularly and fasted often for days at a time, although the writer La Bruyère noted that in chapel the courtiers turned their backs on the priest and knelt facing him, as if they were worshipping him and not God.

For the rest of the morning Louis was usually busy with his Council. On Thursdays, however, he would receive people he specially wanted to see, such as his gardeners or architects. Sometimes for relaxation he might summon writers to read to him or musicians to play for him. He was very fond of music. Sometimes he wakened to the sound of a band playing in the courtyard beneath his window. He was a good singer and played the guitar, the *lute* and the harpsichord.

At the end of the morning the King would leave his study and make his way back to his private rooms. This was always a good time to catch his eye in order to beg a favour or present a *petition*. It was also when a newcomer at court like yourself might be presented to him. The King would have noticed you all right, for he rarely missed what was going on. If a nobleman was away from court for any time he would ask where he was.

This might be the first time that you had ever seen the King at close quarters. He was considered to be a very handsome man, especially when young, with his *sallow* complexion and dark flashing eyes. His nose was rather big and he was probably much shorter than you might think from seeing his portrait. It was his huge wig and high-heeled shoes that made him seem much taller than his 5 feet 4 inches (1.6 metres). Most people were tongue-tied and frightened when they met the King, but he could soon put them at their ease if he wanted. He could also freeze people with a cold stare, but he was usually most polite to women, bowing slightly and raising his hat to the humblest chamber maid.

It was now time for the King's lunch. About five hundred people had been busy all morning preparing it. Louis had a healthy appetite. His sister-in-law recalled seeing him devour at one sitting four bowls of assorted soups, a whole pheasant, a partridge, a large dish of salad, two thick slices of ham, some mutton cooked in gravy, a plate of pastries, all followed by fruit and some hard-boiled eggs.

The King generally ate alone or with the Queen. The nobles had to stand back and watch at a distance in silence. The food had already arrived in specially heated containers from the kitchen far away across the courtyard. The meal was served with the greatest ceremony. Three servants took eight minutes to pour and serve a glass of wine, and after each course the King would gently moisten his fingers on a napkin solemnly presented to him between two silver plates.

In good weather the afternoon was usually spent out of doors. First the King would change his clothes, again watched by members of the court. Louis was always very clean, putting on fresh underwear three times a day. On some days he would simply go for a walk in the Palace gardens with ladies of the

Here you see the King and his courtiers out hunting near Paris at Vincennes

Left: *Louis XIV dressed in ceremonial robes about the year 1701. Notice how everything in the picture seems to make him look very powerful—the rich robes, the high-heeled shoes and the way he is standing. Can you see anything else that is meant to make you feel that this is a great king?*

court; on other days he would play croquet. In summer he would take them for a picnic, in winter they would all go skating. At least once a week he would go out stag-hunting or shoot game depending on the time of the year, bagging as many as 250 birds in one day.

On wet days the King might spend the afternoon indoors in the company of the lady who happened to be his mistress. Throughout his life Louis had many mistresses, perhaps because his wife, Marie-Thérèse, was so dull. For many years his chief mistress was Madame de Montespan, a witty and beautiful woman who was the mother of several of his children. Eventually, however, Louis grew tired of her, especially when it was found that she had been dabbling in witchcraft. Besides, she rarely washed and grew terribly fat. His next mistress was a 55

Louis XIV's wife, Marie-Thérèse

quiet, dignified lady, Madame de Maintenon, who was governess to the royal children. When the Queen died in 1683 Louis secretly married her, much to everyone's surprise.

EVENINGS AT COURT

On Mondays, Wednesdays and Thursdays Louis entertained his courtiers to an evening 'apartement' (reception). The evening began with a play or sometimes an opera or concert. Two of the King's favourite playwrights were Molière and Racine. Molière was best known for his comedies and Racine for his tragedies. The King's favourite musician was Jean-Baptiste Lully, an Italian who first came to France as a kitchen servant and rose to be conductor of the King's orchestra. Lully wrote many pieces of music and composed as many as sixteen operas for the King. Everybody loved his beautiful tunes. According to the King's sister-in-law, 'Court and town sing the Lully *arias*

Louis and his courtiers watching a play at Versailles

that have pleased the King, and they are hummed by every cook in France'. Perhaps you know one of his most famous songs, 'Au clair de la lune'.

As well as musical entertainment there was dancing – stately *minuets* and livelier *quadrilles* – and card playing. Nobles played for huge stakes, and one lady was said to make a living out of playing with the Queen because she was such a dreadful player. The King seldom played cards but enjoyed a game of billiards. All the while music from a small orchestra wafted over the laughter and lively chatter as refreshments were served from tables piled high with all kinds of exciting dishes. What would madame like? An iced *sorbet*, perhaps, or a cup of that new drink from the East that everyone is talking about called coffee?

Not everybody enjoyed the King's receptions. Many were bored, like the King's sister-in-law who described them as 'an absolutely intolerable experience'. Another lady of the court

57

Dancing a minuet at Versailles in 1682. Notice the lighting, the fashions and the refreshments that are just being served

wrote that because of 'the crowds and the overwhelming heat the pleasures of the French court were mixed with much discomfort'. She was not referring only to the entertainments. You had only to live at Versailles for a short time to see that all comfort was sacrificed for the sake of appearance and etiquette. Chimneys were made low so as not to spoil the look of the Palace roof line and as a result courtiers coughed and choked because of the smoking fires. They shivered in winter and sweltered in summer because shutters would have spoiled the appearance of the large windows. Many suffered from sore legs and aching backs because everybody had to stand in the presence of the King unless they were playing cards. Think how sickening it must have been paying compliments to the King all the time. In old age when he complained of having no teeth to chew his food, a courtier exclaimed, 'Teeth, Sire? Who has teeth these days?'

Louis worked very hard at keeping his nobles occupied. In his memoirs he wrote, 'The people enjoy *pageantry* and display. In this way we retain their loyalty and devotion, sometimes more effectively, perhaps, than by just rewards and benefits.' This is why there were so many festivities. A royal wedding, the birth of a royal baby, the visit of a foreign ruler, were all excuses for lavish celebrations, with banquets, masked balls, pageants, fireworks displays and sailing in *gondolas* on lakes and canals by candlelight.

Whatever the occasion, however, evenings always ended in the same way with the ceremony of the 'coucher', in reverse order to the 'lever' of the morning, as the King got ready for bed with his chief courtiers in attendance. Finally after he had climbed into bed and had dismissed his last courtiers he would be all alone, except for his valet, whose last duty was to lay out some food – three loaves, two bottles of wine and three cold dishes – just in case the King should feel hungry in the night. The time would be about 1.30 a.m. The King's day was over.

The day was not over for everybody at Versailles, however. The royal guards were still on duty outside the King's bedroom, and servants were busy cleaning and preparing food in the kitchen for the next day. About 25,000 people lived at Versailles and they had all to be fed and kept clean. Without them the King and his courtiers would not have been able to live in such splendid surroundings.

LE ROY DANS SON CONSEIL
ARBITRE DE LA PAIX ET DE LA GUERRE

5 *The King at Work*

The King did not spend all his time enjoying himself. In fact he got through a lot of hard work. It was hard work simply keeping his nobles busy performing all sorts of useless duties for him. But court ceremonial took up only a small part of the King's day. Most of it was spent attending to the business of ruling the country.

Louis often referred to his 'métier du roi', his trade as a king, and he took it very seriously. 'One must work to reign,' he often used to say. He never spared himself. Knowing how sadly his education had been neglected when he was a boy during the Wars of the Fronde, he shut himself away for hours studying Latin so that he would be able to read the reports sent in by his ambassadors in foreign lands. He planned out very carefully what he would do every day. 'Give me an *almanac* and a watch,' said Saint-Simon, the courtier, 'and I will tell you what the King is doing even if I am 300 *leagues* away.'

Every morning Louis would hold a meeting of one or other of the councils that helped him to govern the country. These councils were made up of ministers who gave him advice and looked after such matters as finance, foreign affairs and defence. Louis chose ministers whom he could trust to do what he wanted. All of them belonged to the middle class and were keen to please the King in order to get on. Louis knew (and so did they!) that if they disobeyed him he could easily dismiss them and replace them with others. Proud members of ancient families, who had advised French kings for centuries, were less

Left: *Louis with his councillors. How can you tell that they will have to do as they are told?*

easy to dismiss, which is why Louis did not choose them as ministers.

Council meetings often went on well into the afternoon because Louis paid close attention to everything to do with the government. He would listen to reports, sign edicts, hear complaints about unfair tax-collectors, and deal with many other matters brought up by his councillors. He would always listen to their advice but he did not always take it. For the first eighteen years of his reign France was ruled in his name by his chief minister, Cardinal Mazarin. In 1661 Mazarin died and straight away Louis made it clear that he would have no more chief ministers. At a meeting of his chief council he said,

> Gentlemen, hitherto I have been content to let my affairs be managed for me. In future I shall be my own prime minister. You will help me with advice, when I ask for it. I order you to seal no documents without my orders, to sign nothing without my consent.

Thus Louis was the government of France and no one had the right to challenge anything he did. How could they when everybody knew that Louis had been appointed by God to rule? Louis was what is often called an absolute monarch. Long after he was dead people said that he had once summed up his position in the words, 'L'Etat, c'est moi' ('I am the State'), but there is no evidence that he ever actually said them.

In order to be a successful ruler Louis had always to be sure that he knew what was going on and that his orders were carried out. He therefore depended a great deal on the officials in different parts of the country who were his special representatives. They were known as Intendants and there were about thirty of them. Each was in charge of a particular district, known as a *généralité*. Their main job was to bring all the provinces, with their different laws and customs, more firmly under the King's control. They reported on how the country was being run. And so, if you were an Intendant, you might have to tell the King how the nobles were behaving, whether or not the judges were being fair, and how well taxes were being collected. After years of weak government and civil war most people were probably quite glad to be ruled by a strong king like Louis XIV.

Louis had some very able men to help him rule France. None was more able than Jean-Baptiste Colbert. As well as being in charge of the royal finances he looked after nearly every government department except the army and foreign affairs.

Colbert was not popular, and if you had lived at Versailles you would easily have seen why. Madame de Sévigné referred to him as 'the North Wind', another courtier called him 'the Man of Marble'. He rarely smiled, always dressed in black and was said to prefer water to wine. The nobles despised him because of his humble beginnings. He was born in 1619, the son of a draper in Reims, although he liked to boast that he was descended from a certain fourteeth-century 'valiant knight, Richard Colbert, known as the Scot' from Inverness. He was such a snob that he even put up a black marble tombstone to this imaginary ancestor in a church in Reims. The nobles disliked him also because unlike so many of them he had got on as a result of his own hard work, and went on working hard all his life. Every morning he arrived at his office at half past six and stayed there reading letters, dictating letters, and going over the King's accounts for eighteen hours a day. He once wrote, 'I take no holiday, I have no pleasure or amusements, my whole time is spent on business, for what I love is work.'

This is why Colbert got on so well with the King. He was also very modest and allowed the King to take all the credit for the work that he did. In 1661, when Louis first appointed him to look after his finances, there was plenty of work to do. The country was exhausted after the years of fighting at home and abroad. The Government was deep in debt and had already spent the money that had still to come in from taxes for the next two and a half years. Harvests had been so poor that many farmers could pay neither rent nor taxes. Trade was bad: 63 merchants were importing more than they exported, which meant that goods from abroad had to be paid for in gold, thus leaving less to be used for money at home. Altogether it was a very gloomy time indeed for France. Yet within ten years all this was changed: France had become the strongest and most prosperous country in Europe, largely thanks to Colbert.

Jean-Baptiste Colbert, Louis XIV's chief minister for many years

Colbert had first to bring some order into the country's finances. How irritated he must have been by the inefficient way taxes were collected! Out of the 83 million livres that people paid out in taxes only 31 millions actually reached the royal treasury: the rest went into the pockets of the tax-collectors. Of course, much more money could have been collected in the first place if only so many people had not been exempt from paying taxes, such as high civil servants and members of noble families, the very ones who could best afford to pay. It was impossible to force such powerful people to pay taxes, so Colbert had to find other ways of collecting more

Ship-building, an example of how Colbert tried to make France prosperous

money for the Government. He therefore reduced the high rates of interest paid to those people who lent money to the government; he persuaded many tax-collectors to give up the money they had wrongfully taken, and he cut down on the number of civil servants who were exempt from taxes.

He saved money in other ways too. He gave the Government its first proper system of accounting: the amount of money it intended to spend in a year was balanced against what it expected to get in from taxes. Since he was careful with his own money Colbert hated to see anybody else's money being wasted. He also despised those people at court who did not do any work. He discovered, for example, that out of the 46,000 jobs in the departments of justice and finance only 6,000 were really necessary; the rest were mere sinecures, so he abolished them. You can imagine how much more unpopular this made him at court! Colbert increased the government's income by making more money out of the royal estates, for example, by selling timber from the royal forests. Altogether, as a result of Colbert's careful management the country's *revenue* doubled between 1661 and 1667 to 63 million livres.

Colbert realised that he could get in even more money for the King by increasing France's prosperity. There was hardly any industry, except for some cloth-making and it was in a bad way. Metal goods had to be imported, including pewter plates and mugs which came from England. Yet Colbert knew that France could be the richest country in Europe on account of its size, its climate, its fertile soil and the skill of its many hard-working inhabitants. In a letter to Cardinal Mazarin some years earlier Colbert had already shown he knew how this could be done:

> We must create or re-create all industries, even luxury industries: a system of *protection* must be established by means of customs *tariff*; trade and traders organized into *guilds*. Transport of goods by sea and land must be restored, colonies developed and bound by financial ties to France; all barriers between France and India must be broken down and the navy strengthened to give protection to our merchant shipping.

With great enthusiasm he set about putting these ideas into practice.

Industry was built up with money from the King in the form of grants or loans at low rates of interest. Manufacturers revived old industries, such as weaving and lace-making. New industries were started, many by foreign craftsmen who were specially invited to settle in France and teach Frenchmen what to do. Soon you could have seen metal-workers and miners from Sweden, weavers and paper-makers from Holland and glass-blowers from Italy, all busy in different parts of the country. At Abbeville a Dutchman, Jan van Robais, was manager of the most up-to-date cloth factory in Europe.

Colbert took a personal interest in all these new industries. He made sure that they had always a supply of cheap labour by ordering orphans and children of the poor to be sent to work in the factories as apprentices. He ensured that manufacturers would always be able to sell their goods by granting many of them *monopolies*. He also protected them from cheap foreign competition by putting high customs duties on foreign imports so that customers would buy the less expensive French goods. Colbert wanted people to buy French products because of their high quality, however, and ordered Intendants to set high standards of workmanship for the workers in their districts. Inspectors were sent round to make sure that these rules were carried out, and so if you were an inefficient clock-maker, let us say, you might end up standing in the *pillory* with a faulty clock hanging round your neck! About a hundred special factories were put up in the name of the King. These royal factories turned out luxury goods of the highest quality, such as *porcelain* at Sèvres and tapestries at Gobelins.

Roads and bridges were built and repaired, rivers dredged and widened and the number of toll stations cut down: there were forty on the river Rhône. A canal was cut, the Canal du Midi, to link the Atlantic with the Mediterranean.

You might have thought that everybody would have been grateful to Colbert for the prosperity he was bringing to France. Instead he made many enemies. Rich merchants and manu-facturers complained about all the regulations they had to obey, and said they would be better off without him. Workmen grumbled about having to give up some of the sixty holy days in the year which Colbert abolished in order to get more work done. The nobles did not help him much. They refused to invest their money in his business schemes. Colbert tried to get the King to persuade the nobles to give up their snobbish ideas about trade and industry but without much success. Most nobles preferred to invest their money in buying land or jobs in the civil service to pass on to their sons and grandsons. As a result French trade and industry in the time of Colbert was held back because of shortage of capital.

COLBERT AND FRANCE OVERSEAS

At times Colbert must have wished he had been born a Dutch-man. In Holland the highest in the land saw the value of trade and were glad to take part in it. Colbert admired the Dutch so much that he tried to copy their methods of becoming rich.

Much of Holland's wealth came from the sea. Dutch

merchants were the world's errand-boys. Their ships could be found in every part of the world carrying goods from one port to another. The money they got from this carrying trade made Holland the richest country in the world for its size.

Colbert aimed at winning the carrying trade for France. It was a difficult task because France had far fewer ships than Holland. In 1669 he estimated that the Dutch had from 15,000 to 16,000 ships, France under 600. He therefore charged foreign ships *harbour dues* and granted *bounties* to French ships that went in for foreign trade. He encouraged the building of new ships. To defend the merchant navy Colbert increased the size of the King's navy too, from thirty old and leaky ships in 1661 to 176 in 1683.

The Dutch made a great deal of money also from their colonies in America, India and the Far East. Every year their great ships came back laden with sugar from Brazil, cotton from India, spices from Indonesia and fine silks, tea and porcelain from China and Japan. Holland was the only country at this time which had such prosperous colonies, and so the merchants of Amsterdam made great profits from selling these goods to customers all over Europe. Dutch trade with countries overseas was carried on by great trading companies. Colbert therefore set up French trading companies: the Company of the West Indies to handle trade with America, the Company of the East Indies to trade with India and the Far East, the Levant Company to bring home rare goods from the East by way of the ports of the eastern Mediterranean. The Company of the North brought back essential supplies of timber, hemp and pitch for ship-building. These companies were all set up with government money – the East India Company alone received 6 million livres in loans, and were granted a monopoly of French overseas trade. They brought in much wealth, although they were never able to compete with the Dutch because they never had as much capital.

In order to develop France's overseas trade Colbert aimed at developing those French colonies that had already been set up in the West Indies and North America. In Canada he intended that the tiny trading-posts along the banks of the St Lawrence river should grow into thriving cities in a vast empire called New France. The colonists there would produce valuable raw materials for sale back home and buy in return the manufactures of France's new industries, just like the colonists of Holland and England. New France, Colbert hoped, would bring in even more wealth to France and add to the glories of Louis XIV.

Compared with the Dutch and English the French had been very slow to colonise North America. Their colonies had been set up by small private companies of enterprising gentlemen and adventurers. But few Frenchmen wanted to go out as settlers. Most Frenchmen in North America were fur-traders, or 'coureurs du bois' (runners of the woods) as they were called. They went out into the dense forests to trap wild animals and came back with rich pelts of beaver, squirrel and mink to sell at trading-posts such as Montreal and Quebec.

Colbert saw that an empire could not be built simply on fur-trading. New France needed settlers to go out as farmers and merchants to clear the forest, cultivate the soil, set up towns and develop trade on a big scale. First of all the colonies had to be brought under the control of the King. This was done in 1664. Soon, at government expense, shiploads of peasants, accompanied by soldiers and priests, were being sent out to colonise Canada.

The colony flourished. In 1663 there were only about 2,500 French people in Canada; by 1672 there were over 10,000 of them, with their own 'seigneurs' and priests, their own Governor, Intendant and bishop, just like back home. Their chief town, Quebec, was a busy little port with a harbour and dockyard.

Louis XIV never showed much interest in the empire in America that Colbert built for him. His mind was taken up with events in Europe and he could not see how valuable colonies might be to France. As a result he did not send out enough troops to defend them nor did he encourage people with money to invest it there. Few emigrants could be persuaded 69

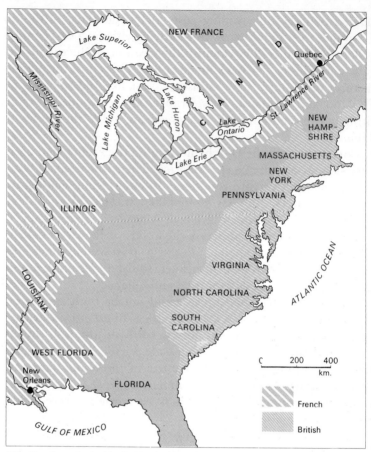

The French empire in North America that was started in the time of Louis XIV. Louisiana was named in honour of the King

to go out to settle, and therefore trade between Canada and the home country did not bring in all the wealth that Colbert expected. By 1683 New France stretched in a curve north-eastwards from the mouth of the Mississippi to the mouth of the St Lawrence river, but little came of this vast empire in Colbert's time. But his plans to extend France's overseas trade did produce benefits. By the end of Louis XIV's reign France's overseas trade was worth 200 million livres a year, and two-thirds of this was in exports. Colbert's work had not been in vain.

Colbert performed many other useful duties. As Superintendent of Buildings he transformed Paris and made it a more fitting capital for France under Louis XIV. Many of the dirty and *dilapidated* old parts of the city were pulled down to make way for new streets and squares. New suburbs appeared, such as the Faubourg St Martin and the Faubourg St Honoré, with their broad avenues and imposing mansions. A start was made in demolishing the old city walls, so that by 1715 Paris was surrounded by broad, tree-lined walks along the top of the outer defences or 'boulevards'. The Champs Elysées was laid out as a delightful park. Paris was made much safer and healthier. Streets were properly paved. Drainage and water supplies were improved and many public fountains were set up. Tradesmen who blocked the streets with their materials and refuse were made to pay heavy fines. At night the streets were illuminated with over 6,000 reflecting lanterns, so that Paris became known as the best-lit city in Europe. Until this time Paris had had only sixty policemen to cope with a city of about half a million inhabitants. These included 40,000 beggars and countless numbers of thieves and vagabonds who used to terrorise the streets at night. Colbert organised a police force of forty-eight *commissaires* and 800 sergeants, which made Pairs much more law-abiding than it had been before.

One of the many things the police had to do was to *censor* books and newspapers in case they said anything that might offend the King. Louis disliked any criticism and liked only praise; anybody who spoke out or wrote anything against him was liable to land in jail. As a result, no one was allowed to print anything without Colbert's consent. This shows you that the King tried to control not only what his subjects did but also what they thought.

As Minister of Fine Arts Colbert was able to make sure that most writers wrote only what the King wanted. He did it 71 partly through the French Academy. This was a body of famous writers, set up earlier in the century, whose main work was to watch over the French language to keep it free of words that were foreign, out-of-date, vulgar or coarse. In 1694 it finally produced a dictionary of the French language, one of the first in the world, in which all unwanted words, such as 'cracher' (to spit), 'vomir' (to vomit) and many other everyday words, were left out because they were unfit to be used in decent company. It was considered a great honour to become a member of the French Academy, especially since pensions were paid to its members, and Colbert arranged that only those writers who pleased the King should be elected. In 1671 he paid out 100,500 livres in prizes and pensions to French writers. Musicians, painters and scholars were also encouraged in this way.

Louis XIV was genuinely interested in the arts. He greatly helped the French theatre. In 1673 Colbert brought various theatrical groups together to form one professional company that was supported by the King, the Comédie Française. Its purpose was to put on plays by the best French dramatists, performed by the best French actors. In this way the standards of the French theatre became the highest in Europe.

Like everything else he did Colbert's help for the arts was supposed to add to the glory of Louis XIV. Everybody realised this and many writers and artists resented being so much under the King's control. They longed to be free to do what they wanted and try out new ideas. This was not easy when they depended so much on pleasing the King.

You will have seen how much Colbert did for Louis XIV and you can judge for yourself how much good he did for the French people. Despite his great achievements, he died in 1683 a bitterly unhappy man. He had failed to carry out many things dear to his heart, such as giving France a code of law and a system of taxation that would have applied to the whole country. He had had to give up or change many of his plans because his many enemies turned the King against him. But without Colbert's loyal service Louis XIV's reign would not have been nearly so glorious.

6 The King at War

Although Louis valued highly all that Colbert did to make France wealthy he was not really interested in such things as finance, trade and industry. This is why he left them so much in Colbert's hands. Louis was much more interested in foreign affairs, *diplomacy* and war, matters which were more likely to bring him lasting fame and glory. He once wrote: 'My *dominant passion* is certainly love of glory.' By 'glory' he meant becoming famous for doing noble deeds like heroes of ancient times such as Alexander the Great and Julius Caesar. He wanted to bring glory to France, so, having restored order and brought prosperity, he was determined to make it the most powerful country in Europe.

Louis knew that he could do this only by going to war. This did not worry him. War to him was something glorious. In 1661 although most people in France were sick of war the nobles were keen to fight. Some of them still believed that fighting was what nobles were born to do, and when there was no war at home they went off to fight against the Turks, who were very warlike at this time. Louis was sure that he would always have plenty of men willing to fight for him as long as they were paid; and he knew that he would have enough money to pay them thanks to Colbert's careful handling of his accounts.

Louis soon discovered that his army was in a very bad state. One of his ministers described it as 'a republic composed of as many provinces as there are lieutenant-generals'. The army was not the King's army at all, its generals could do almost what they liked. Officers were not appointed by the King but by two colonels-general, one for the *cavalry* and the other for the

This is the sort of thing that ill-disciplined troops were allowed to do at the start of Louis's reign

infantry. Compared with the Dutch army and the English army in the time of Cromwell, the French army was very poorly managed indeed. When the colonel-general of infantry died in 1661, however, Louis took charge of the army himself and set about reforming it.

The man Louis appointed to carry out this work was François Michel le Tellier, better known as the Marquis de Louvois. Like Colbert, Louvois was eager to build up France's power and influence. Just as Colbert was doing it by making the country wealthy, Louvois aimed at doing it by going to war. Few people liked Louvois. He was a rough, bullying sort of man, who did not care what he did as long as he got his own way. But since he was also loyal and very efficient, Louis trusted him with a great deal of responsibility. Louvois was appointed Secretary of State for War in 1677, in succession to his father, who had held the post for the past twenty years and with whom he had been working. Between them Louvois and his father made the French army the best in Europe.

THE WORK OF LOUVOIS

If you had been a French soldier at this time you would have seen changes taking place in the army all the time. You would have become accustomed to wearing a uniform. Until about

74

1670 soldiers wore ordinary clothes, with simply a sash or rosette of their captain's colours to distinguish them from other soldiers. By 1683 most French soldiers were dressed in uniform, light grey for the infantry, and either red or blue for cavalry regiments.

Louvois,
Louis's Minister of War

You might have to learn how to use a new kind of *musket* known as a 'fusil'. The old musket was heavy to carry and awkward to use. You had to load it with ball and powder, prop it up on a wooden fork stuck into the ground, and then fire it with a fuse that you had first to light by striking tinder. The new musket was lighter to handle and it fired more quickly, too, by means of a *flintlock* on the gun itself. It was useful for fighting at close quarters, simply by slipping over the muzzle the newly invented bayonet.

75

A musketeer, carrying his musket with its pivot, along with a lighted fuse. Round his body hangs his bandolier complete with charges full of gunpowder

Living conditions in the army were made slightly better. Instead of having to survive during campaigns on hard, dry biscuits that you carried on a bandolier slung across your body, you might now get soft, newly baked bread to eat. This was thanks to a new portable oven that could bake enough bread for six days at a time. Your pay was still the same, 5 sous a day with 1 sou 6 *deniers* taken off for food, but at least you got paid more regularly and according to a fixed scale. Most soldiers were still quartered in inns or private house, although some of you were now living in those new barracks being built. This was supposed to stop you terrorising the countryside, stealing peasants' food and making off with the local women. In fact, discipline was tightened up in many ways, although you were less likely to be flogged if you landed in trouble. When you were wounded or fell sick you were better looked after in the new field hospitals. In Paris there was even a huge new home for old soldiers, known as the Hôtel des Invalides.

There was certainly no shortage of recruits for the army. In the past it had only been in times of famine that men were driven to 'join the bread wagons', as they called joining the army. Now volunteers flocked to fight in the French army from all over Europe. Perhaps, as they marched off to war whistling tunes specially written for them by Lully the King's composer, French soldiers knew that with a bit of luck they might rise to become an officer one day.

This was because officers as well as the rank-and-file, were affected by Louvois's reforms. They could no longer buy their commission below the rank of captain; and new senior ranks of major, lieutenant-colonel and brigadier were introduced for poor but efficient officers who deserved promotion. Officers had also to undergo regular periods of training and drill, which was unheard of earlier. Those who objected were simply persuaded to retire to their estates or were dismissed the service.

An inspector-general named Martinet went round making sure that the new regulations were being carried out. Martinet was commander of the King's regiment, and his discipline was so strict that all young officers had to serve under him before they joined their own regiments. The methods he used to train these young men earned him such a reputation that anybody who was a strict disciplinarian came to be known as a 'martinet'.

Louvois greatly improved the army's organisation. He increased the number of infantry regiments, until by 1691 the ratio of infantry to cavalry was five to one. Until this time the cavalry had been considered the most important branch of the army: foot soldiers had been thought only good for softening up the enemy before the cavalry charged and scattered them. During the wars of the later seventeenth century, however, there were fewer pitched battles in which the cavalry could take part. Victories were more often won by massed ranks of infantry all firing their muskets at the one time. Most of the fighting that took place now consisted of long and sometimes very dreary sieges, in which gunners and engineers played the most important part. Until now they had hardly belonged to the army at all, but were supplied by civilian *contractors*.

77

Louvois brought them under the King's control. He set up the corps of engineers and founded schools to train gunners. Even the cavalry underwent change. The men were equipped with *sabres* instead of swords for slashing downwards at their enemy in battle. Officers still preferred to fight in the cavalry because it was considered the smartest and most dashing branch of the army, but the King insisted that they should first serve in the infantry.

Possibly the greatest of all Louvois's achievements was to set up a proper system of supply for the army. Like Napoleon Bonaparte over a century later, Louvois knew that an army marches on its stomach. He therefore set up throughout France permanent storage depots to keep the army supplied with food, ammunition and equipment. French armies were therefore able to fight long campaigns far away from their base, fully supplied from a nearby depot. They could also fight throughout the winter instead of having to disband and muster again in the spring, much to the surprise of their enemies.

Louvois did not always find it easy to get his ideas carried out. Generals hated taking orders from him because he was a civilian. What did he know of military matters, they said? And as for the special Intendants for the army who carried out his orders, military commanders looked on them as glorified clerks and interfering busybodies. In spite of such difficulties Louvois went ahead and modernised the French army. It was thanks to him that Louis was so successful in all the wars he fought.

AT WAR WITH THE DUTCH

France was at war for most of Louis XIV's reign, first with Spain, later with the Dutch, and finally with nearly all the countries of Europe. His most persistent enemies were the Dutch. Louis loathed them because they seemed to stand for everything he disliked. 'Maggots governed by cheese merchants', he called them. They elected wealthy citizens to govern them while he believed that people should be ruled by kings appointed by God. They were mainly Protestant while he was a leading Roman Catholic. What made matters worse, they were tremendously rich and yet did not show off their wealth. As one French writer put it: 'They are great masters of the Indian spices and the Persian silks, but wear plain woollen cloth and feed upon their own fish and roots.' Even their chief of state, the Grand Pensionary, 'dressed in a plain coat and went on foot like one of the townspeople, followed by a servant dressed in grey, who carried a red velvet bag in which were the most important papers in Europe'. And to think it was people like these, much of whose tiny little country was under sea-level and had only recently been won back from the sea, who were daring to stand up to the most powerful ruler in Europe!

The Dutch, you see, had recently dared to interfere in Louis's affairs. In 1668 he was fighting Spain to gain control of Spanish provinces that lay on France's northern and eastern borders: the Spanish Netherlands (modern Belgium) to the north, and the Franche Comté to the east. You can see these places on the map on page 81. Louis wanted these provinces to make France safe from invasion. The Dutch, on the other hand, were afraid that if Louis captured the Spanish Netherlands he might go on to attack them. They therefore formed an alliance with the English and the Swedes to stop Louis. This made him furious because he had to make peace. He gave the Franche Comté back to Spain but held on to towns he had captured in Flanders. Having been prevented from gaining all the glory he had expected from a war with Spain, Louis determined to take his revenge on the Dutch. His ministers gave him full support. Colbert, as you know, was eager to take away Dutch trade. Louvois wanted to crush them so that his armies could take over the whole of the Spanish Netherlands. All of them urged Louis to make war on Holland.

Louis planned his war against the Dutch with great care. As in the war against Spain, he told his ambassadors to win over foreign rulers to his side. French *diplomats* were the best in Europe. They were also supplied with plenty of money to pay spies and bribe rulers to do what Louis wanted. The ruler who received the most money from Louis was Charles II of England. Louis paid him £741,985 over a period of eight years. To win 79

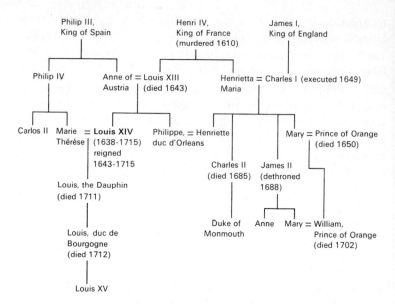

From this family-tree you can see how closely Louis XIV was related by marriage to the royal families of Spain and Great Britain

him over to his side against the Dutch, Louis sent over to England in 1670 his sister-in-law, Henriette, Duchess of Orleans, who was also Charles II's favourite sister. The real purpose of the mission was kept so secret that even gossipy French courtiers knew nothing about it. Charles and his sister made an agreement known as the Secret Treaty of Dover, by which the English King said he would join in a war against the Dutch when Louis was ready, and receive in return about £166,000. Other countries, including Sweden and some of the German states, were also brought into Louis's web of alliances.

By the spring of 1672 his preparations were complete. He had assembled an army, 120,000 strong and fully equipped, four times bigger than any other army of the time, and led by some of the most experienced generals in Europe. Against him stood the Dutch army of 30,000 ill-fed and badly clothed men, their leaders divided among themselves. Some, led by William, Prince of Orange, were all for standing up to Louis XIV, others followed the Grand Pensionary, John de Wit, and his brother, Cornelius, who had done all they could to keep the peace.

The war started when England declared war on Holland and the English and French fleets sailed out against the Dutch fleet. Louis began his fighting against the Dutch without any warning when he sent his armies through the lands of the Bishop of Münster, one of his German allies. Three weeks later he joined them, a striking figure in high jackboots, long leather gloves and a hat with a large red plume. Many of his courtiers went with him to share in the glory. They included an artist to paint pictures of the battles and a historian to write a glowing account

This map may help you to follow Louis' wars against Spain and the Dutch in the Netherlands

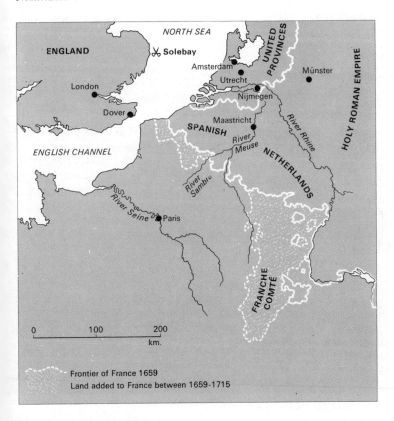

of the whole campaign. Louis lived under canvas, ate the same food as his officers and shared, for a short time, some of the discomforts of an army on the march.

You can follow what happened on the map. The French armies moved swiftly down the valleys of the rivers Sambre and Meuse and then struck across country to the river Rhine to where it was only about 50 metres wide and shallow enough to cross. The Dutch were waiting at the other side, but at last the French soldiers were able to clamber ashore. By evening a bridge of light boats had been put into position and Louis was able to cross the Rhine in triumph.

The Dutch armies retreated, the French advanced westwards and occupied all the southern part of the *United Provinces.*

Louis XIV at the crossing of the river Rhine. Pick out the King with his officers, the French army gathering on the river bank and crossing over to the other side

Victory over the Dutch seemed certain. But instead of marching straight on to Amsterdam, the chief town in Holland, Louis ordered his armies to halt. This turned out to be a grave mistake, for it gave the Dutch time to defend their country in a most dramatic way.

Like other parts of the United Provinces the land around Amsterdam was very flat and low-lying because it had been reclaimed from the sea. High dykes kept back the sea and the flow of water from the drained land was controlled by a system of canals, dams and *sluices*. The Dutch pierced the dykes and opened the sluices. The French now found all the land between them and Amsterdam flooded to a depth of over a metre. The fields were covered with water. The farms were deserted. Nearly all the roads were impassable. The French advance had been halted. The only way to attack Amsterdam now was by sea, but the French and English fleets had been defeated by the Dutch at Solebay off the coast of Suffolk. Holland was saved and Louis had been cheated of total victory.

The Dutch leaders, John and Cornelius de Wit, asked for peace, saying that Louis could keep all the land he had conquered in the United Provinces. Louis, however, would grant peace only on his terms. As well as keeping the land he had captured, he demanded that the Dutch should pay him 24 million livres, grant French merchants special trading privileges, and send to his court every year an ambassador with a medal commemorating France's victory over them. The furious Amsterdam mob had its answer to these harsh terms: it seized the unfortunate de Wit brothers, who had always wanted to keep on the right side of Louis, and hanged them. The French terms of peace were turned down and the Dutch people rallied to resist the invader.

The Dutch leader was William, Prince of Orange, who had only recently been appointed *Stadtholder* to command all their forces on land and sea. He was a pale-faced, slight young man of only twenty-two who suffered much ill-health, but he became Louis's most stubborn enemy. And so, under William of Orange the Dutch went on fighting.

84   *Louis's bitter enemy, William, Prince of Orange, leader of the Dutch*

Unable to make any headway towards Amsterdam because of the floods, in the summer of 1673 Louis turned southwards to take the important fortress of Maastricht, which stood on the road along which help might come for the Dutch from the German states. It was a heavily fortified town with four sets of *concentric ramparts* and ditches. The governor refused to surrender so Louis brought up a huge army of 26,000 infantry and 19,000 cavalry with 58 cannon to besiege it.

If you were a commander of an army besieging a fortress at this time you could either starve the defenders out or else take it by storm after blowing up the walls. To do this, you had first to send out your *sappers* to dig a long narrow trench right up to the outer defences and set off mines underneath. Then, amid the smoke and the dust you led your men charging into the town over the fallen rubble. It was not an easy job, because while your men were busy digging their trench the enemy would be firing at them from behind their walls.

Louis planned the siege of Maastricht differently. A bright young engineer in his army, Sébastien de Vauban, had learnt from the Turks of a new way to attack a town. Instead of running a single trench, Vauban ordered his men to dig a line of wide trenches in a zig-zag pattern right up to within thirty metres of the town's outer defences. From these trenches troops could protect the sappers with covering fire as they planted their mines in the forward trench. After the sappers had dug and mined for nearly a fortnight the attack on Maastricht began.

Among those taking part in the siege was a young Englishman, twenty-two-year-old Captain John Churchill who later became famous as the great English general, Marlborough. Eager to win glory for himself, he was one of about fifty English soldiers serving in the French army under the Duke of Monmouth, son of Charles II. Louis showed great interest in his English troops and saw to it that Monmouth and his men took part in the storming party during the final assault on the town.

The attack was timed to start at 10 p.m. Imagine how

Churchill and his men must have felt as they waited in their trench. At last the King gave the signal for them to move off. Flashes of cannon-fire lit up the darkening summer sky as Churchill and the others made for the stout outer defences of the town gateway. *Grenades* by the thousand exploded all round them. Losses were heavy in the close musket-fire. At last, after bitter hand-to-hand fighting Churchill was able to break free and plant the French standard on top of the battered *parapet*. For the rest of the night the Englishmen held off the attacking enemy until a relief force took over.

The English soldiers were resting in their tents next day about noon when suddenly a messenger came running to say that the Dutch were trying to re-take the captured positions. Rousing his men and without waiting to enter the zig-zag trenches, Churchill joined Monmouth in charging across the open ground. When they reached the gateway the fighting was at

This shows you the intricate pattern of defences that Vauban worked out to defend fortresses at this time

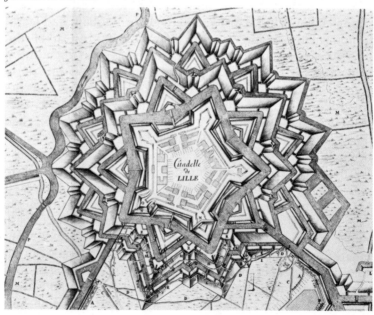

This is a cross-section of the outer defences of a fortress

its height. They were joined by the King's musketeers, led by the famous d'Artagnan. When d'Artagnan fell dead with a shot in the head, Monmouth rallied the attackers on. Helped by about 500 fresh troops they finally succeeded in taking back the positions won the night before. Some weeks later when he saw that further resistance was hopeless, the governor of Maastricht finally surrendered.

Meanwhile, Louis gave his engineer Vauban the job of rebuilding Maastricht's defences. This gave him the chance to carry out new ideas of his own in fortifying a town. He strengthened the outer wall with a series of jagged strongpoints placed at regular intervals, each giving covering support to the others on its flanks. The usefulness of these new fortifications was tested two years later when the Dutch gave up trying to take back the town after a siege lasting forty-one days. Louis' siege of Maastricht was therefore an important stage in the development of ways of both besieging and defending towns.

THE REST OF THE WAR

Louis's war against the Dutch dragged on for another five years. William of Orange persuaded other rulers, including the Emperor, the King of Spain and some German princes, to come into the war on his side.

By 1764, however, the French as well as the English and Dutch had had enough. Representatives from the countries at war met in the Dutch town of Nijmegen, to discuss ways of bringing the fighting to an end. Once again Louis's diplomats showed how skilful they were, keeping the peace talks going to get the best terms for France. Carefully they played on the many 87 differences among the Dutch and their allies. For example, they offered more generous terms of peace to the Spaniards so as to stir up trouble between them and the Dutch.

At long last the Treaty of Nijmegen was drawn up and signed. Louis insisted on it being written in French instead of Latin, the usual language for treaties. By the treaty, Louis agreed to withdraw his troops from the United Provinces and to abolish the heavy customs Colbert had imposed on Dutch imports. He also agreed to give up some of the towns he had taken earlier in the Spanish Netherlands, although this was only to round off his northern frontier and make it easier to defend. The King of Spain handed over to France the Franche Comté, and the Emperor gave him some towns in southern Germany on the eastern bank of the river Rhine.

The Place des Victoires in Paris, with the statue of Louis XIV that was put up to celebrate his victories

Judge for yourself how much of a victory the war with the Dutch had been for France. Louis himself was very proud of what he had achieved. People called him 'Louis the Great', wrote poems and erected statues and monuments in his honour. Everywhere statesmen agreed that he was the most powerful ruler in Europe. At the same time they wondered what he would try to do next. Having got what he wanted by waging war would he be content now to live in peace?

7 Postscript

It was soon clear that Louis was not content to live at peace after 1678. Having got his own way by using force he went on using force to add to his kingdom. Finally the rulers of Europe thought Louis was becoming too powerful and they banded together to stop him. When next he went to war in 1688 he found himself fighting nearly all the countries of Europe. The war lasted nine years. After a break in the fighting it started all over again in 1701 and went on until 1713. Peace came with the Treaty of Utrecht, but unlike earlier treaties Louis had signed this one was not a victory for him. The victors were the Emperor, the Dutch and the British. Louis had to give up land he had taken, but as you can see from the map he was still able to hold on to those lands he had conquered earlier.

The cost of the wars was colossal. Losses in men were enormous. In one battle alone, Malplaquet in 1709, France lost about 13,000 men, the enemy 20,000. Louis's ministers racked their brains to think of ways of paying for the wars. Old taxes were raised and many new ones were brought out, including one on playing games of cards. All sorts of titles and jobs were specially invented and put up for sale, such as official refuse collector and captain of the local crossbowmen. The country was bled white with taxes. As usual the poor suffered most. Years with bad harvests brought rocketing prices and heavy unemployment. Thousands died of starvation. The population fell by about two million.

Most historians agree that Louis reached the peak of his reign around 1680. Until then he was fairly cautious in what he did and was successful in war. After then he had no great ministers to guide him. (Colbert, remember, died in 1683). As well as becoming involved in costly wars he did some foolish things, such as *persecuting* his Protestant subjects, the Huguenots. Many were brutally put to death, others fled to Germany, Holland and England. Since many were highly skilled craftsmen they made France poorer and the countries where they settled all the richer. Wherever they went they made enemies for Louis. In the later part of Louis's reign he had few outstanding soldiers. French armies were less often victorious and were beaten by generals such as the Duke of Marlborough and the Austrian Prince Eugène. Fewer clever men came to Louis's court. He could no longer afford to pay them on account of the wars. Versailles was still as splendid as before but few people chose to live there. It was so dull. Under the influence of Madame de Maintenon, Louis became very strict in his ways: there was very little merry-making and courtiers discovered that it was fashionable to appear religious. Most nobles preferred to live in Paris.

Louis XIV endured much suffering in his last years. He lost his son, two grandsons and one great-grandson within about a year. His splendid health was ruined. Surgeons almost broke his jaw taking out two bad teeth, and doctors nearly killed him with their bleedings, drugs and purges, trying to relieve his stomach disorders. Finally his body became covered with dark blotches. *Gangrene* in his leg set in and he died in September 1715, three days before his seventy-seventh birthday. The reign of the 'Sun King' was over.

Things to Do

1. Make a collection of stamps commemorating famous people and events in French history and find out more about them. Mount a display of the stamps and write short notes explaining the importance of the people and events displayed.
2. Here are some suggestions for model-making: a peasant's house; a nobleman's castle; a nobleman's 'hôtel'; a fortress designed by Vauban. Try to dress dolls in the fashions of the seventeenth century using the pictures in this book as a guide.
3. Imagine you are on holiday in France in the seventeenth century living with a nobleman's family. Write a letter home telling about your life there, describing the house, its grounds, and the different people you have met.
4. Write a guide-book to Paris in the time of Louis XIV, pointing out the places a visitor might like to visit. Be sure to warn your readers about the drawbacks as well as telling them about the pleasures of Parisian life.
5. 'This is what I want for my new Palace ... ' Using this as an introduction, write an imaginary conversation between Louis XIV and his advisers about the building and decoration of the Palace of Versailles.
6. Here are some suggestions for adventure stories: a young foreign student in Paris at the time of the Wars of the Fronde describes what happened when he fell in with some nobles who were plotting to kidnap the young King; a maidservant at Versailles saves Louis XIV from a terrible scandal and is suitably rewarded; a young nobleman is cheated of his inheritance, joins a troupe of strolling players, meets Molière, is kidnapped and sent off to Canada.
7. Write a short account of what kind of a man you think Louis XIV was, first as if you were a writer hoping to receive a pension from him, and then as a Huguenot writer who has been forced to flee to Holland after 1685.
8. 'Army life isn't what it used to be when I was a lad.' As an old

soldier, describe what it was like to fight in Louis XIV's army and say what you think of the changes being made by Louvois.

9. Here are some novels about France in the seventeenth century that you may like to read:

ARTHUR CONAN DOYLE, *The Refugees* (Huguenots in France and America);

ALEXANDRE DUMAS, *The Three Musketeers* and *Twenty Years After* (both about the period before Louis XIV); *The Man in the Iron Mask*, *Vicomte de Bragelonne*, and *The Black Tulip* (about Holland in 1672);

RENÉ GUILLOT, *The King's Corsair*, translated by Geoffrey Trease (a tale of piracy in the reign of Louis XIV);

MARGARET IRWIN, *Royal Flush: the story of Minette* (about Henriette, Louis XIV's English sister-in-law).

How do we know?

It is possible to learn a great deal about France in the time of Louis XIV because there are so many sources of information written by people living at the time. Life at court was described by people who lived in it and were interested in what went on. For example the Duc de Saint-Simon who was fascinated with everything he saw Louis do, wrote it all down in his Memoirs. Madame de Maintenon did not write memoirs but she did write many letters. So did the King's sister-in-law, a German princess named Liselotte. She was not always happy at court and had to watch what she said, but she got rid of some of her bad feelings by writing to her friends. More valuable in many ways as sources of information are the Letters of Madame de Sévigné. She wrote not only about life at court but about life in Paris and in the different parts of the country that she visited.

It is always much more difficult to find out about the life of ordinary people in the past for the simple reason that until recently most people could not write. Even if they had known how to write they probably would not have thought their life worth writing about. This means that we have usually to rely on what other people, upper-class people, wrote about them, either directly or indirectly in stories and plays. La Fontaine's 'Fables' tell us about the life of ordinary people and so do the plays of Molière, especially about servants and their masters, well-to-do Parisians.

Peasants seldom appear in plays except as simple fools. They are mentioned in official documents of the time, such as the reports sent in to the King by Intendants, but simply as a great wretched mass of people, rarely as individuals. Foreign visitors were not interested in them either, although both John Locke and John Evelyn, who kept journals of their travels in France, occasionally mentioned what they saw of country life.

Peasants as individual people come to life from a most unexpected source of information, the dusty, yellowing pages of documents kept by clerks and village priests. Recently historians have been patiently studying records of everyday happenings that throw a great deal of light on what life was like for ordinary people. Registers of marriages, baptisms and deaths tell about such things as what times of the year couples got married, the size of families, and common causes of death. Rent rolls and inventories of estates tell about the value of land, what crops were grown, what animals were kept and how well off peasants really were. The peasants from the Île de France you read about in Chapter 1 really did exist. They have stepped out of the pages of records kept at the time.

Easier to lay hands on than all these sources of information are books written by historians, based on the sources. There are a great many of them. Here are a few you may like to read if you want to find out more about the France of Louis XIV:

ALFRED APSLER, *The Sun King,* Messner, 1965

CHARLES BLITZER, *Age of Kings,* Time-Life International, 1967 (excellent for pictures)

JOHN LAURENCE CARR, *Life in France under Louis XIV*, Batsford, 1969

NANCY MITFORD, *The Sun King,* Harper and Row, 1966

Glossary

abbot, head of a monastery

almanac, book of information about days of the year

apothecary, old name for a chemist

arcade, passage with arched roof, often with slopes along one or both sides

aria, song for soloist in an opera

bounty, gift of money

cannibalism, eating of human flesh

cardinal, prince of the Roman Catholic Church who helps to elect the Pope

cavalry, soldiers on horses

to censor, to cut out anything critical

commissaire, French magistrate who helps to prevent crime

commission, right to be an officer

concentric, having a centre in common

confronted, brought face to face

congregation, gathering of people

contractor, person who carries out work for you at a fixed cost

cornice, plaster moulding round a ceiling

cravat, kind of neck-cloth

denier, old French coin worth a twelfth of a sou

devotion, here means 'on a religious subject'

devout, religious

dilapidated, fallen into decay

diplomacy, arranging relations with other countries

diplomat, person who arranges relations with other countries

dominant passion, what a person loves the best

dowry, money or goods given with a bride at her marriage

edict, law given by a king

effectually, well

ell, old measure of length equal to just over a metre

entrée, dish at dinner served between main courses

Estates, here, kind of parliment for French province made up of local
   nobles
etiquette, accepted rules of behaviour
fallow, uncropped
financier, man who deals in large sums of money
frieze, band on wall decorated with painting or sculpture
Frondeurs, people who fought against the King in the wars of the
   Fronde
gangrene, blackening of the body,first stages of death
garlic, plant with strong taste used for flavouring food
gondola, long narrow boat
grenade, small bomb thrown from the hand
guild, company of craftsmen or merchants
harbour dues, payments for ship using harbours
harpsichord, old-fashioned keyboard instrument similar to piano
hemp, plant grown for making coarse cloth or rope
inclinations, abilities
infantry, here, foot soldiers
lavish, extravagant, over-generous
league, old measurement of distance equal to about five kilometres
lineage, family ancestors
living, occupation in the Church to support a clergyman
livre, old French money worth 20 sous
lute, old-fashioned musical instrument with strings which was played
   like a guitar
major-domo, head servant of wealthy household
Mass, church communion service
memoirs, description of events remembered by the author
minuet, slow stately dance
monopoly, sole right to trade in something
musket, old-fashioned gun with a long barrel
ornate, fancy
pageantry, splendid display
parapet, defence of earth or stone
parlement, important court in France
pavilion, jutting-out part of a building at right angles to main part
to persecute, to punish a person for his religious or political opinions
petition, written request for something to be done
pewter, grey metal made up of lead and tin
philosopher, here, learned man
pillory, wooden frame with holes through which minor offenders
   stuck head, hands and legs, for punishment by ridicule

poaching, stealing of wild animals, birds or fish

porcelain, very fine china

posterity, descendants or successors

precedence, order of doing things according to rank

protection, helping the making of goods in a country by putting taxes on imports

quadrille, square-dance for four or more couples

rampart, mound of earth used for defence

rape-oil, oil made from plant that was used for greasing

revenue, income of a country

rue, French for street

sabots, wooden shoes in France

sabre, heavy one-edged sword, slightly curved, used by cavalry

sallow, pale, yellowish colour

salon, French for large room in a house for meeting people

sapper, soldier who builds fortifications and lays mines

sedan chair, covered chair for one carried on two poles

seigneur, French for lord, owner of land or landlord

serf, peasant who must work for the owner of the land on which he lives

sluice, a gate for controlling the flow of water in a canal

sorbet, flavoured water ice

sou, small copper coin worth a twentieth of a livre

Stadtholder, chief officer in United Provinces

sumptuous, very rich in decoration

superior, here, person in charge of land who receives payment from others who use the land

symmetrical, evenly balanced in design

tariff, form of tax on goods imported or exported from a country

tithe, tenth part of what a person owned paid to the Church

toll, charge made for passing over a bridge or road etc

turret, small tower

United Provinces, seven states that had broken away from Spanish rule in the sixteenth century led by Holland, nowadays called the Kingdom of the Netherlands

valet, personal man-servant

wattle and daub, interwoven twigs plastered with clay or mud

weather-vane, revolving pointer fixed to a high roof or tower to show which way the wind blows

wench, country girl

wrought, worked or made